Your Ri
1998-99

Your Rights

A GUIDE TO MONEY BENEFITS FOR OLDER PEOPLE

1998-99

Sally West

BOOKS

Age Concern would like to thank the Department of Social Security for its comments on the text. The author also thanks colleagues in Age Concern England Policy Unit for their contributions.

Published by Age Concern England
1268 London Road
London SW16 4ER

© 1998 Age Concern England

Twenty-sixth Edition

This edition prepared by Sally West

Editor Ro Lyon
Production Vinnette Marshall
Typeset by GreenGate Publishing Services, Tonbridge, Kent
Printed in Great Britain by Bell & Bain Ltd, Glasgow

A catalogue record for this book is available from the British Library

ISBN 0-86242-255-8

Bulk orders
Age Concern England is pleased to offer customised editions of all its titles to UK companies, institutions or other organisations wishing to make a bulk purchase. For further information, please contact the Publishing Department at the address on this page. Tel: 0181-679 8000. Fax: 0181-679 6069. E-mail: addisom@ace.org.uk

CONTENTS

Further Information **127**

INTRODUCTION

This book provides information about the main financial benefits available for older people. Most of the social security rates given apply from the week beginning 6 April 1998.

Your Rights is divided into five parts. The first section gives details about pensions and retirement, and the second section is about financial help for those on low incomes. The third section covers benefits for disabled people and their carers, while the fourth gives information about other types of financial help, including the system of help towards paying for residential and nursing home care.

Many of the subjects covered in *Your Rights* can be complicated, and the book aims to explain them as simply as possible. However, it cannot cover all situations and circumstances. If you need more information, the fifth section gives details about obtaining relevant Department of Social Security (DSS) leaflets, factsheets prepared by Age Concern and contacting other local and national sources of help. There is also an index and a summary of main benefit rates on page 152.

Please note that although some older people have young families, benefits for children are not covered in this book.

Where you live

All the information covered in *Your Rights* applies to people living in England and Wales. It also applies to Scotland except where differences are pointed out in the text.

Although there are separate social security systems in the Isle of Man and Northern Ireland, the social security benefits available are generally the same. However, there may be some differences in the sources of financial help discussed in the section 'Other Financial Benefits'.

The national Age Concern organisation in Northern Ireland produces its own edition of *Your Rights* which highlights any differences between the systems.

For further information or advice relating to older people living in Scotland, Wales and Northern Ireland, contact Age Concern Scotland, Cymru or Northern Ireland – the addresses are on page 138.

For more information on pensions and benefits for people living abroad, either permanently or temporarily, you should contact your local Benefits Agency (social security) office (if you are currently in this country) or the Pensions and Overseas Benefits Directorate, Tyneview Park, Whitley Road, Benton, Newcastle Upon Tyne NE98 1BA; this is the part of the Benefits Agency that deals with pensions and benefits paid abroad. It produces a series of leaflets covering social security arrangements with countries outside the UK including Jersey, Guernsey and the countries of the European Union.

Keeping up to date

This book is based on information available at the beginning of March 1998 and should apply until the beginning of April 1999. If you would like to be kept up to date with any major changes during the year, please fill in the form on page 137.

At the time of writing we do not know what the Chancellor will announce in his March 1998 Budget. It will not necessarily affect the information in *Your Rights* as state pension and benefit rates were announced in December 1997. However if you would like a summary of the March 1998 Budget proposals please ring 0800 00 99 66 and ask for a Budget update sheet.

A number of proposed changes are mentioned in *Your Rights*. If you need information about the latest position or you have questions on any specific points in the book, please write to Age Concern England at the address on page 138 or ring 0800 00 99 66.

A new edition of *Your Rights* will be available in April 1999 – please let us know if you have any comments or suggestions.

Pensions, Widows' Benefits and Retirement

This part of Your Rights *contains information about State Retirement Pensions. There is also a section on early retirement, which describes the benefits available to people who leave work before State Pension age, and another which looks at the effect on State benefits if you choose to work after pension age. In addition there are details about widows' benefits; the Christmas Bonus (paid to people receiving a State Pension or certain other benefits); the procedure for appealing against a social security decision; and occupational and personal pensions.*

RETIREMENT PENSIONS
(TAXABLE)

To qualify for the State Retirement Pension you must have reached pension age (60 for women, 65 for men) and fulfil the National Insurance (NI) contribution conditions.

Your pension may consist of a Basic Pension plus an Additional Pension (based on contributions after April 1978) and a Graduated Pension (based on contributions between April 1961 and April 1975). You will receive an extra 25p when you reach the age of 80. You may also receive extra pension if you defer drawing your pension. These different parts of the pension are explained below.

Whether you are entitled to a State Pension or not, you may be able to claim other benefits such as Income Support, Housing Benefit and Council Tax Benefit, which depend on your income and savings.

See social security guide NP 46 about Retirement Pensions.

Equalisation of State Pension age

Parliament has passed legislation to equalise State Pension age at 65 for both men and women. This is to be phased in over ten years starting in 2010. No one born before April 1950 will be affected by these changes.

BASIC PENSION (TAXABLE)

The Basic Pension is paid at the same rate to everyone who has fulfilled the NI contribution conditions. The full weekly rates are shown below:

Single person	£64.70
Wife on husband's contributions	£38.70
Married couple on husband's contributions	£103.40
Married couple (if both paid full contributions)	£129.40

Who qualifies?

You will receive the full basic rate of pension if you have paid, or been credited with, NI contributions at the full rate for most of the years of your working life. If you have not paid enough, you may get a reduced pension or you may not get a pension at all (see 'Your contributions', pp 7–10).

Normally you need to have satisfied the contribution conditions in your own right; but married women, divorcees or widowed people may be able to claim a pension on their spouse's or ex-spouse's contributions, as explained in the following pages.

Pensions for married women

If you are a married woman and you have paid full contributions for all of your working life, you should be entitled to the Basic Pension of £64.70 a week when you become 60. If you have paid full contributions for only part of your working life, you may be entitled to a reduced pension. However, any years when you were paying the married woman's reduced-rate contributions will not count towards a pension.

If you are 60 or over but have not paid enough contributions for a pension in your own right, you cannot get any Basic Pension until your husband draws his. When your husband draws his pension, you should claim the married woman's pension, which will be £38.70 a week if your husband has a full contribution record.

At the age of 60 you may be entitled to a pension on your own contributions. If this is less than £38.70 a week, it will be made up to a maximum of £38.70 a week when your husband draws his pension. However, if your own pension is more than £38.70 a week, you cannot get any extra pension based on your husband's contributions.

Married women who worked in the 1940s

If you worked before the present National Insurance scheme started in 1948, perhaps during the war years, you may have been paying contributions which could count towards a pension now. The rules are complicated but sometimes women find that even if they have not worked for many years, the contributions they made earlier on can help them qualify for a partial pension. However, if you are already receiving a pension or another benefit, for example a pension based on your husband's contributions or a Widow's Pension, you may not be entitled to anything more.

Example

Catherine Hewitt worked from 1946 until 1956 when she got married. When she became 60 she could not draw a pension on her husband's contributions because he was only 55. However, she was entitled to a small pension based on the contributions she had paid.

If you think you might be entitled to a pension, contact your local Benefits Agency (social security) office with details of when you paid contributions, your past employment, your maiden name and, if possible, your NI number.

Increases for dependants

Dependent wives

If you are under 60 when your husband draws his pension (at 65 or more), he may be able to claim for you as a dependant, and his pension will be increased by a maximum of £38.70 a week. However, your husband will not receive any increase for you if you receive certain State benefits of £38.70 or more. It may also be affected by any earnings you have.

If you live with your husband, he will not be able to receive the increase if you are working and earn more than £50.35 a week (after certain expenses connected with work have been deducted). Any occupational or personal pension you receive will be counted as earnings. If you do not live with your husband, he will not be able to receive this increase if you earn more than £38.70 a week.

If your husband has been receiving the increase since before 16 September 1985, an older rule may apply. In this case the earnings limit will be £45.09. If you earn more than this amount, the increase is gradually reduced.

Dependent husbands

If you are a married man and your wife is receiving a State Pension, she may be able to get an increase for you of up to £38.70, provided you are not earning more than £50.35 a week (£38.70 if you do not live with your wife). However, she can get this increase only if she is receiving Incapacity Benefit with an addition for you immediately before she starts to draw the State Pension. Your wife will not receive any increase if you have a State Pension or certain other benefits of £38.70 or more.

Pensions for divorced and separated people

Divorced people

If you are divorced but do not qualify for a full pension based on your own contributions, you may be able to use your former spouse's contribution record to increase the amount of Basic Pension you receive to a maximum of the single person's pension of £64.70 a week. Before 6 April 1979 this applied only to women who divorced before reaching pension age (60). You are not entitled to your former spouse's Graduated or Additional Pension.

You can substitute your former spouse's contribution record for your own from the start of your working life up until your divorce or just for the period of your marriage.

If you get divorced before pension age, you may need to pay further contributions after your divorce to qualify for a Basic Pension.

If you get divorced after pension age and are receiving the married woman's pension, you may be able to use the rules outlined above to get a full pension.

People who remarry

If you remarry before pension age, you cannot claim a pension on your former husband's or wife's contributions. However, if you remarry after pension age you will not lose a pension based on your previous spouse's contributions.

See social security leaflets CA 10 and WRP 2, which give information for divorced women.

Separated women

If you are separated and do not qualify for a pension on your own contributions when you reach 60, you may be able to claim the married woman's pension of up to £38.70 a week when your husband claims his.

Retirement Pensions for widows and widowers

Widows

If you were under 60 when your husband died and you have not remarried, you may be entitled to the State Pension based on his contributions and/or your own, once you reach pension age.

If you were 60 or over when your husband died, and not receiving the full Basic Pension, you may be able to use his contribution record to bring your Basic Pension up to a maximum of £64.70.

You will receive his Additional Pension plus your own up to the level of the maximum Additional Pension for a single person. This will be adjusted to take into account any time you and/or your husband were 'contracted out' of the State Additional

Pension scheme, as explained on pages 16–18. You will also receive half of his Graduated Pension as well as any based on your own contributions.

Once you are drawing the State Pension at age 60 or over, you can remarry or live with a man as his wife without losing a pension based on your previous husband's contributions.

Widows should also see pages 25–26 on the Widow's Payment and Widow's Pension.

Widowers

If you were widowed on or after 6 April 1979 and do not have enough contributions of your own, you may be entitled to a Retirement Pension based on your wife's contributions provided you were both over pension age when she died.

You may also inherit half your wife's Graduated Pension and add her Additional Pension to your own up to the maximum Additional Pension for a single person. If you do not fulfil the above conditions, perhaps because you were widowed before age 65, once you reach pension age you may be able to substitute your wife's contribution record for your own in order to increase your Basic Pension up to a maximum of £64.70 a week.

Your contributions

This section explains the contribution conditions for the Basic Pension. Your contribution record will depend on the NI contributions you have paid and any 'credits' you received for periods when you could not work. There are two conditions that you must meet in order to receive a pension.

The first condition is that you have paid sufficient contributions during at least one year in your working life since 6 April 1975 or paid at least 50 flat-rate contributions at any time before 6 April 1975. Credited contributions cannot count towards this first condition.

The second condition is that to receive a full Basic Pension you must have paid or been credited with contributions for most of the years of your working life. To receive any Basic Pension at all you must have a minimum number of years' contributions.

Whether you will get a full pension depends on your 'working life' and 'qualifying years', and whether your contribution record has been protected by 'credits' and/or 'Home Responsibilities Protection'. These terms are explained below.

If you are more than four months away from pension age, you can check whether you have paid enough contributions to get a full pension by completing form BR 19, obtainable from your local Benefits Agency (social security) office.

Both men and women aged 80 or over who have not paid enough contributions for a Basic Pension might qualify for the non-contributory pension described on page 19.

How are contributions paid?

Since April 1975 employed people have paid contributions as a percentage of earnings, and these are collected with Income Tax.

Self-employed people pay flat-rate contributions each week which count towards the Basic Pension. If your taxable income is over a certain amount, extra contributions will be collected with your Income Tax.

Which contributions count?

If you paid the married woman's or widow's reduced-rate contributions, these do not count towards a pension in your own right.

Contributions made abroad may help you qualify for the Basic Pension provided the country where you worked has a reciprocal agreement with the UK.

See social security leaflet NI 38.

Working life

Your 'working life' is the period on which your contribution record is based. This normally starts in the tax year (ie 6 April to 5 April) when you were 16 and ends with the last full tax year before your 60th (women) or 65th (men) birthday. A woman reaching pension age now has a working life of 44 years and a man reaching pension age now has a working life of 49 years.

However, if you were over 16 when the National Insurance scheme started in 1948, you may have a shorter working life – see social security guide NP 46.

Qualifying years

A 'qualifying year' is a tax year in which you have paid (or been credited with) enough contributions to go towards a pension.

Since 1978 a 'qualifying year' has been one in which contributions are paid on earnings which are the same as, or more than, 52 times the weekly lower earnings limit. (Between April 1975 and April 1978 the qualifying earnings were 50 times the lower earnings limit.)

The lower earnings limit is the level at which you start to pay NI contributions on all of your earnings. This tax year, 1998–99, the lower earnings limit is £64 a week. If you earn less than this, you do not pay contributions towards a pension.

Before 1975 working people paid contributions by weekly stamp. To work out your qualifying years before 1975, all your stamps (paid and credited) are added up and divided by 50, rounding up any that are left over – but you cannot have more qualifying years worked out in this way than the number of years in your working life up to April 1975.

See social security leaflets NI 196 (on contribution rates), CA 01 (NI for employees), CA 02 (NI for self-employed people).

Credits

If you are under pension age (60 for women, 65 for men), you may receive a credit in place of an NI contribution for each week you register for Jobseeker's Allowance and are seeking work or you are unable to work because you are sick or disabled or you are receiving Invalid Care Allowance. Men aged 60–64 who are not paying contributions will normally receive credits automatically even if they are not ill or signing on as unemployed. However, men cannot get these automatic credits for any tax year during which they are abroad for more than six months.

Late and voluntary contributions

If there are periods when you will not be paying contributions, perhaps because you will be abroad, you may want to consider paying voluntary contributions to protect your pension record. If there are gaps in your contribution record, it is sometimes possible to pay late contributions. However, these must normally be paid by the end of the sixth tax year after the one in which they are due. Ask at your Benefits Agency (social security) office if you need advice.

See social security leaflets CA 08 (on voluntary contributions) and CA 07 (on late contributions).

Calculating your pension

To be entitled to a full Basic Pension, about nine out of every ten years of your working life have to be qualifying years. This means that women with a working life of 44 years will need 39 qualifying years for a full pension. Men with a working life of 49 years will need 44 qualifying years for a full pension.

If you are not entitled to the full Basic Pension, you may get a reduced one provided you have at least a quarter of the qualifying years you need for a full pension.

Example

Christina Paretsky was born on 10 August 1938 and was 16 in 1954. Her working life runs from 6 April 1954 to 5 April 1998, a total of 44 years. To receive a full Basic Pension, she needs 39 or more qualifying years. If she has worked and paid contributions for only 20 years of her working life, she will receive about half the Basic Pension.

Home Responsibilities Protection

Home Responsibilities Protection (HRP) started in 1978 to protect the contribution record of people caring for a child or a sick or disabled person.

You cannot get HRP for the years when you were looking after someone before April 1978. A married woman or widow cannot get HRP for any tax year in which she, if she was working, would only be due to pay reduced-rate NI contributions.

You are entitled to HRP if you meet any of the following conditions, or a combination of them, for a whole tax year (but note that the rules changed in 1988 for the third condition):

- You get Child Benefit for a child under 16.
- You get Income Support because you are looking after someone and therefore do not need to register for Jobseeker's Allowance.
- For at least 35 hours a week you look after someone who receives, for a minimum of 48 weeks in the year, Attendance Allowance, the middle or highest rate of the care component of Disability Living Allowance, or Constant Attendance Allowance. For tax years before 6 April 1988, the allowance had to be paid for 52 weeks.

If you get Invalid Care Allowance, you will normally be getting credits towards your pension so you will not need HRP, although you cannot get credits if you retained the right to pay the married woman's reduced-rate contributions.

How to work it out

HRP makes it easier for you to qualify for a Basic Pension. Each year of 'home responsibility' will be taken away from the number of qualifying years you need to get a full pension. However, HRP cannot normally be used to reduce the number of qualifying years to below 20.

Example

Eileen Smith, who was born in 1938, started work at 16 and paid full contributions for 30 years until 1984 when she gave up work to look after her mother. She was still caring for her mother when she became 60 in 1998 so her pension was worked out in the following way:

Working life	44 years
Number of qualifying years needed for a full pension	39 years
Number of years of HRP	14 years
Number of qualifying years needed for a full pension after taking away years of HRP	25 years

Normally Eileen would need to have paid contributions for 39 years in order to receive a full pension. However, because her 14 years of HRP reduce the number of qualifying years she needs to 25, she is entitled to the full Basic Pension although she has paid only 30 years of contributions.

When to claim

HRP will be given automatically if you qualify under the first two conditions described above. You do not have to claim.

You must claim HRP if you qualify under the third condition – because you are looking after someone who is getting one of the allowances mentioned above, such as Attendance Allowance – or if you qualify under one condition for part of the tax year and under another for the rest of the year. Ask for claim form CF 411 from your Benefits Agency (social security) office.

How to claim your pension

About four months before you reach pension age you should be sent a claim form. If you have not received one three months before your birthday, contact the local Benefits Agency (social security) office. Fill in the claim form as soon as you receive it. A married woman claiming a pension on her husband's contributions will need to fill in a separate form.

You may decide not to draw your pension at 60 (women) or 65 (men) in order to gain extra pension, in which case, when you wish to start claiming the pension, you should contact your local office well in advance. Deferring your pension is explained on pages 20–22.

Once you reach the age of 65 (women) or 70 (men), you should claim your pension as you will gain no further increases.

At the time of writing, if you make a late claim for your pension, it can be backdated for up to three months. However, the Government intends to restrict backdating to one month from June 1998.

How your pension is paid

There are two ways to have your pension paid. You may choose to collect it each week at a post office, in which case your pension is paid one week in advance. If you cannot get to a post office, someone else can cash your pension for you. The pension book explains how this is done.

At the time of writing, people who choose to collect their pension at the post office receive an order book, which is cashed weekly. However, all pension and social security benefit order books will be gradually phased out and replaced by benefit payment cards. This change is due to take place over the next two or three years. You will take your card to the post office and a computerised system will tell the post office staff how much is due to you in pension or other benefits. The Department of Social Security (DSS) says that the changes will be well publicised and everyone receiving a pension or benefit by order book will be sent information about the payment card. For more information contact Age Concern England at the address on page 138.

If you prefer to have your pension paid into a bank, building society account, or post office account, you can have it paid directly by 'automated credit transfer'; the money will then normally be paid in arrears and you can choose to receive it either four-weekly or quarterly. However, if you receive Income Support this can be paid together with your pension by automated credit transfer, weekly in advance.

Pay-day for anyone who started to draw their pension before 28 September 1984 is normally Thursday. For people who retired after that date, pay-day is usually Monday, although if your spouse is already receiving a pension on Thursday, you can choose to have yours on the same day. You cannot receive any pension for days of retirement before your first pay-day.

Most pensions of £5 a week or less (£2 a week for awards of pension made between July 1987 and October 1996 and £1 a week for awards prior to July 1987) are paid once a year, in December, in arrears. If you requested payment by automated credit transfer, you will be paid by that method; if you requested payment by order book, you will be paid by crossed payable order.

See social security leaflet NI 105 (payments into bank or building society accounts).

Going abroad or living there

If you receive your pension by weekly order book and are going abroad for less than three months, you can cash your pension orders when you come home. However, a pension order cannot be cashed more than three months after the date printed on it. If you are going abroad for longer, tell your local Benefits Agency (social security) office well in advance so that your pension can be paid into a bank or other account while you are away. Alternatively, you may arrange for your pension to accrue and be paid in one lump sum on your return.

If you do not receive your pension by weekly order book, you do not need to tell your local office unless you are staying abroad for more than six months. You can, if you wish, arrange to receive your pension in the country where you are staying. If you remain abroad, the annual pension increase will be paid only if you are living in a European Union country or in a country with which the UK has special arrangements.

Contact your local Benefits Agency (social security) office or the Pensions and Overseas Benefits Directorate, Tyneview Park, Whitley Road, Benton, Newcastle Upon Tyne NE98 1BA.

Going into hospital

If you go into hospital, you will receive your full pension for up to six weeks. After that, if you are single, your pension is usually reduced by £12.95 and if you are still in hospital after one year it will be reduced to only £12.95 a week.

If you are married and your husband or wife is at home, he or she will be considered as your 'dependant'. When you have a dependant, your pension is reduced by £25.90 a week after six weeks in hospital. After a year, your pension will be reduced by a further £12.95 a week. You will normally be paid £12.95 of the pension and, if you agree, the rest will be paid to your dependant.

See social security leaflet NI 9.

If you disagree with a decision

If you think that you have been awarded the wrong amount of pension, or disagree with another decision to do with your pension, you can either ask for the decision to be reviewed or appeal against it. Further details about reviews and appeals are given on pages 28–30.

ADDITIONAL PENSION (TAXABLE)

The Additional Pension, paid under the State Earnings-Related Pension Scheme (SERPS), started on 6 April 1978 and is based on earnings on which you have paid contributions since then. You may qualify for an Additional Pension even if you are not entitled to the Basic Pension. Employees pay into SERPS unless they have 'contracted out' of the scheme, as explained below.

The Additional Pension is related to weekly earnings from April 1978 until the 5th of the April before your 60th (women) or 65th (men) birthday. Earnings from past years are revalued in line with increases in average earnings. The pension is based on each year's revalued earnings between certain levels which are known as the 'lower and upper earnings limits'. In 1998–99 these weekly limits are £64 and £485 respectively. If you reach pension age before 6 April 1999, your total revalued earnings will be divided by 80 to give the yearly amount of Additional Pension.

Changes to the scheme that will reduce the amount of SERPS people receive are being phased in between 1999 and 2009. So if you reach pension age on or after 6 April 1999 the pension will be calculated in a different way.

For further details about the calculation for people retiring both before and after 6 April 1999 see social security guide NP 46.

Contracting out of SERPS

Instead of paying into SERPS, people can join a 'contracted-out' occupational scheme (if their employer runs one) or take out an 'appropriate personal pension'. (Always take professional advice before taking out an appropriate personal pension.)

If you join an employer's contracted-out occupational pension scheme, this will provide an occupational pension in place of the State Additional Pension and both you and your employer will pay lower NI contributions. If your occupational scheme is not contracted out, you will continue to pay the standard NI contributions and will receive both the full Additional Pension and any occupational pension you are due under the rules of the scheme. An adjustment may be made to your occupational pension in respect of your Additional Pension. Contact the administrator of your scheme for more information. If you join an appropriate personal pension scheme, the DSS makes a contribution direct to your pension provider.

Contracted-out occupational pension schemes and appropriate personal pension schemes have to satisfy certain conditions.

There are two types of contracted-out occupational pension scheme: salary-related schemes and money-purchase schemes. A contracted-out salary-related (COSR) scheme will provide a pension related to your earnings. The minimum amount of pension you will receive based on contributions up to April 1997 is called the Guaranteed Minimum Pension (GMP), which is broadly equivalent to the State Additional Pension you would have received. The system changed for contributions made from April 1997 onwards. Instead of providing a specific GMP, the scheme must fulfil certain conditions in order to be contracted out.

A contracted-out money-purchase (COMP) occupational scheme or an appropriate personal pension scheme gives a pension based on the value of the fund an individual has built up (through contributions and the investment return on these). This is known as your 'Protected Rights'. There is no GMP as such, but your Additional Pension will be reduced by an amount which may be more or less than the pension provided by your scheme.

When you receive details of your State Pension, this will show how much the Additional Pension would be based on your earnings. If you were contracted out of SERPS for any time, the statement will show a 'contracted-out deduction' which takes into account the time when you were not paying into SERPS. The amount of Additional Pension (before the deduction) minus the contracted-out deduction shows how much Additional Pension will actually be paid on top of your State Basic Pension.

For Additional Pension earned from April 1997, the details of your State Pension will no longer show a contracted-out deduction. For any given period of time when you were working, you will earn either Additional Pension or an occupational or personal pension.

It is a good idea to seek professional financial advice before contracting out of SERPS, especially if you are considering entering a money-purchase scheme or taking out an appropriate personal pension. For some people who have contracted out of SERPS, it may be advisable to contract back in again at a later date. Again, you should take advice.

Widows and widowers

A widow can inherit her husband's Additional Pension and add it on to her own. However, this cannot add up to more than the maximum Additional Pension a single person can receive. Adjustments will be made for periods when the husband was contracted out of SERPS. A widow is entitled to half of her husband's GMP (if he was a member of a COSR scheme). A widow whose husband was a member of a COMP or appropriate personal pension scheme will receive a pension from the scheme.

These rules also apply to a widower if his wife dies when they are both over pension age (60 for women, 65 for men).

Social security guide NP 46 gives more details about how Additional Pension is calculated.

GRADUATED PENSION (TAXABLE)

This pension scheme existed from April 1961 to April 1975 and was based on graduated contributions paid from earnings. If you were over 18 during this period and paying graduated contributions, your Graduated Pension (also known as Graduated Retirement Benefit) for the year 1998–99 will be based on the weekly rates shown below:

Women	8.4p for every £9.00 contributions paid
Men	8.4p for every £7.50 contributions paid

This will be paid when you claim your pension, normally with the Basic Pension. However, you can receive Graduated Pension even if you do not qualify for a Basic Pension.

Married women, widows and widowers

If you are a married woman of 60 or over and your husband has put off drawing his pension, you should be aware that any Graduated Pension you receive – however little – may mean that you will not benefit from an increased married woman's pension when your husband draws his pension. See page 22 for further information.

A widow can inherit half her late husband's Graduated Pension, as can a widower whose wife died after 5 April 1979, provided they were both over pension age (60 for women, 65 for men) when she died.

OVER-80s PENSION (TAXABLE)

This is a non-contributory Retirement Pension of £38.70 a week for people aged 80 or over who have no Retirement Pension. For someone who already gets a Retirement Pension of less than £38.70 a week, an Over-80s Pension will be paid to bring that pension up to this level.

To qualify for this pension you have to be living in the UK on the day you became 80 or the date of your claim if this is later, and to have been here for ten years or more in any 20-year period after your 60th birthday. If you have lived in Gibraltar or another European Union country, this may help you satisfy the conditions.

The Over-80s Pension will be counted as income in full for the purposes of Income Support, Housing Benefit and Council Tax Benefit.

See social security leaflet NI 184.

GOING ON WORKING

This section looks at the choices open to people who wish to work after reaching pension age (60 for women, 65 for men). People can choose to claim their pension or to defer it (that is, put off drawing it) in order to gain increases later on.

Working and drawing the State Pension

Once you reach pension age, you can draw your State Pension if you satisfy the contribution conditions. It will not be affected by the amount you earn or the number of hours you work. You should note, however, that if you are claiming an addition with your pension for a dependent husband or wife, this addition could be affected by their earnings, as explained on pages 4–5.

Although your pension will not be reduced because you are working, it is counted as part of your taxable income. Your tax code will be adjusted to take into account any pension (including Additional and Graduated) you receive.

If you carry on working after pension age, you will not have to pay NI contributions. You should receive a certificate of exception from the DSS to give to your employer, who will still have to pay contributions for you.

Deferring your pension

You can choose to defer drawing your pension for up to five years after pension age in order to earn extra pension.

You cannot normally defer a pension after the age of 65 (women) or 70 (men). However, you may be able to do so if you are a married woman of 65 or over with a husband under 70 who is deferring his pension, as explained below. The period for which you defer your pension will be called 'the period of enhancement'.

You do not have to be working to defer your pension but you will not be counted as deferring your pension if you are receiving certain other benefits instead. For example, a woman who decides not to draw her pension at the age of 60 but to continue to claim Widow's Pension until the age of 65 will not gain any extra pension.

Even if you start drawing your pension, it is possible to change your mind and defer it instead. However, this can only be done once. If you are a married man and your wife is drawing a pension based on your contributions, you may need your wife's consent before cancelling your pension as she will have to give hers up too.

Extra Basic Pension

If you defer your pension, it will be increased by about 7.5 per cent a year for each full year that you do not draw it. (If you were deferring your pension before 6 April 1979, you will have earned a smaller increase.) For each week that you defer your pension, it will be increased by 1/7p in the pound, but you must defer it for at least seven weeks to gain any increase.

If you put off drawing your pension for the full five years, it will be increased by about 37.5 per cent. For example, in April 1998, the Basic Pension of £64.70 a week would be increased to about £88.95 a week for someone who had deferred it for five years.

See social security leaflets NI 92 and NP 46.

Extra Additional and Graduated Pension

If you defer drawing your pension, your Additional and Graduated Pensions will be increased in the same way as the Basic Pension.

See social security guide NP 46 for information about the effect of deferring your pension on an occupational pension.

Extra pension for married women

If you are a married woman entitled to a pension on your own contributions and you defer drawing it, the pension will be increased as described previously.

If you are aged 60–64 and entitled to a pension on your husband's contributions, you can defer this to gain an increase. If you are 60 or over and your husband is deferring his pension, you will not be able to draw the married woman's pension. Once he draws his pension, you will both receive increases.

However, your pension on your husband's contributions will not be increased if, while your husband is deferring his pension, you draw another benefit such as Additional Pension or Graduated Pension. It may be better not to draw, for example, a small Additional Pension if your husband is deferring his pension.

Unemployment and sickness

If you have deferred your Retirement Pension, you cannot claim Incapacity Benefit or Jobseeker's Allowance if you become unable to work. This is because neither of these benefits can start to be paid to someone who has reached pension age.

EARLY RETIREMENT AND UNEMPLOYMENT

This section summarises the benefits available to older people who leave work or become unemployed before pension age (60 for women, 65 for men) and explains how to ensure that your Retirement Pension is protected.

Jobseeker's Allowance (JSA) (taxable)

JSA replaced Unemployment Benefit and Income Support for unemployed people in October 1996. There are two elements: contribution-based JSA, which is based on your NI contribution record, and income-based JSA, which is means-tested.

To qualify for JSA you must be:

- under pension age (although if you are aged 60–64 you can claim Income Support instead);
- unemployed or working for less than 16 hours a week;
- capable of and available for work; *and*
- actively seeking work. You must have entered into a Jobseeker's Agreement with an Employment Service adviser, and you must comply with any directions given.

Contribution-based JSA can be paid for a maximum of 26 weeks. The rate for people aged 25 or over is £50.35. There are no additions for dependants. Although in general income and savings are not taken into account, if you have an occupational or personal pension of over £50 a week this will reduce any contribution-based JSA by the amount by which your pension exceeds £50.

Income-based JSA can be paid in addition to the contribution-based JSA or on its own if you do not have sufficient NI contributions or you have already received contribution-based JSA for 26 weeks. To qualify for income-based JSA you must have no more than £8,000 savings and a low income. If you have a partner, his or her income and savings will be added to yours and your partner must either not be in work or be working for less than 24 hours a week on average.

The rules for calculating income-based JSA are similar to those for Income Support described on pages 35–45. If you qualify for income-based JSA you may also get other benefits such as Housing Benefit and Council Tax Benefit and help with NHS costs. If you do not have to sign on in order to receive benefit (eg because you are aged 60 or over or are a carer receiving Invalid Care Allowance) then you should claim Income Support instead of income-based JSA.

A number of schemes have been introduced to encourage people to get back to work. These include a 'Back to work bonus' and the continuation of Housing Benefit and Council Tax Benefit for an extra four weeks after you start work and your JSA stops. Ask at the Jobcentre for further information.

How to claim

You claim JSA from your local Jobcentre, where you will be given a claim pack and an interview will be arranged. Once JSA is awarded you will need to 'sign on' every two weeks.

If you leave work voluntarily without 'good cause' or refuse a job, then you may be disqualified from benefit for up to 26 weeks. You may lose benefit if you accept early retirement, although not if you are made redundant. There are also other ways you may lose benefit. For example, if you do not carry out a Jobseeker's Direction which was reasonable for you to do, you could lose two weeks' benefit.

If you are refused benefit or need help or advice with claiming JSA, contact a local advice agency.

Incapacity Benefit

If you are unable to work because of sickness and are no longer employed, you may be entitled to Incapacity Benefit, depending on your contribution record. See pages 84–89 for details.

Occupational and personal pensions

You may qualify for some occupational pension before pension age (60 for women, 65 for men) if you retire early. You should check with your employer for details.

You can draw a personal pension at any time between the ages of 50 and 75. However, you cannot start to receive an 'appropriate personal pension', paid instead of the State Additional Pension, before pension age.

Income-related benefits

In addition to the types of income described above, such as Incapacity Benefit and occupational pensions, you may be able to receive one or more of the income-related benefits – Income Support, income-based Jobseeker's Allowance, Housing Benefit and Council Tax Benefit. These benefits depend on your income, savings and other factors. Income Support and Jobseeker's Allowance cannot be paid together. You can receive Income Support only if you do not need to 'sign on' for work in order to receive benefit.

Protecting your State Pension

To make sure that you have paid enough contributions to receive a full pension when you reach pension age, check your contribution record by contacting your local Benefits Agency (social security) office.

You will receive credits towards your pension if you are drawing a benefit such as Jobseeker's Allowance or Incapacity Benefit. If you are under 60 and seeking work, it may be worth signing on as unemployed – even if you are not entitled to benefit – because you will receive credits. If you are a man aged 60–64, you will normally receive credits automatically even if you are not ill or signing on as unemployed. However, you cannot get these automatic credits for any tax year during which you are abroad for more than six months. If you are not entitled to credits and have an incomplete NI record, you may want to consider paying voluntary contributions.

WIDOW'S PAYMENT AND WIDOW'S PENSION

This section is aimed at older women; women widowed under the age of 55 or with dependent children should seek further information from a local advice agency. The two benefits described both depend on the husband's contribution record.

Widow's Payment (not taxable)

This is a single lump-sum payment of £1,000; it was introduced in April 1988 and is paid mainly to widows under the age of 60. If you are 60 or over when your husband dies, you will still receive the payment provided he was under 65 or he was over 65 but not receiving the State Retirement Pension.

Widow's Pension (taxable)

If you were aged 55–64 when your husband died (and you had not started to receive a Retirement Pension), you can receive a Widow's Pension of up to £64.70 a week. If your husband had not paid sufficient contributions, you may not get the full amount. You may also receive an Additional Pension based on your husband's earnings since April 1978. Adjustments will be made if there were periods when your husband was contracted out of SERPS because he was a member of a contracted-out occupational pension scheme or an appropriate personal pension scheme.

When you reach pension age (60), you can draw the State Retirement Pension instead of the Widow's Pension or you can remain on the Widow's Pension until you reach 65. The amounts will often be the same, but you may also receive some Graduated Pension with the State Pension. Check with the DSS what the different amounts would be.

The Widow's Pension will not be affected by your earnings. However, if you do not draw your Retirement Pension at the age of 60, you will not earn extra pension unless you give up the Widow's Pension.

If you remarry before you reach 60, you will lose the Widow's Pension. It will also be suspended during any period when you live with a man as his wife. However, if you are 60 or over and receive a Retirement Pension based on your previous husband's contributions, you will not lose this if you remarry or live with someone.

See social security guide NP 45.

CHRISTMAS BONUS

The bonus of £10 will be paid to people who are entitled to one of the State benefits listed below and who are living in the UK or any European Union country during the week beginning 7 December 1998. The bonus is tax-free and has no effect on other benefits.

Who qualifies?

You will get the Christmas Bonus if you are receiving a Retirement Pension; Over-80s or Widow's Pension; Attendance Allowance; Disability Living Allowance (any level or component); Invalid Care Allowance; Industrial Death Benefit; Incapacity Benefit payable at the long-term rate; Severe Disablement Allowance; Income Support (provided you have reached pension age: 60 for women, 65 for men); War Widow's Pension; Unemployability Supplement or Allowance; or Constant Attendance Allowance paid with a War or Industrial Disablement Pension. It is also payable to someone who receives a War Disablement Pension but does not get a qualifying social security benefit if they have reached 65 (women) or 70 (men).

Only one bonus can be given to each person. However, someone over pension age may get an additional bonus for a dependent spouse or an unmarried partner who is over pension age or who reaches pension age during the week beginning 7 December 1998 but is not entitled to the bonus in their own right, as long as the relevant conditions are satisfied.

How it is paid

There is usually no need to claim, as the bonus is paid automatically. Depending on the way your pension is normally paid, the bonus will be added to your pension to collect at the post office, paid into a bank or building society account, or sent by giro cheque. If you think you are entitled to the bonus but do not receive it by the end of December, inform your local Benefits Agency (social security) office.

REVIEWS AND APPEALS

This section gives brief details about what to do if you disagree with a decision about a benefit or pension. It applies to many benefits but not to discretionary Social Fund payments, Housing Benefit, Council Tax Benefit or the medical conditions for disability benefits. For more information, see the relevant sections.

At the time of writing proposals are being considered which will make major changes to the system for reviews and appeals. These are intended to be introduced after April 1999. For more information contact Age Concern England at the address on page 138.

Most social security decisions are made by adjudication officers. If you disagree with one of their decisions, you can ask for it to be reviewed or take an appeal to a Social Security Appeal Tribunal (SSAT), which is independent of the DSS. There are also 'Secretary of State decisions', as explained below.

When you receive information about whether you have been awarded a benefit and how much you will get, you should also receive details about what to do if you disagree with the decision. If you want to challenge a decision, it is often useful to get advice from a local agency such as a Citizens Advice Bureau. They may be able to help you write to the DSS, prepare your case, or perhaps represent you at a tribunal.

Reviews

You can ask for a decision about your benefit to be reviewed at any time, if you think that the adjudication officer did not have all the facts or misunderstood the information supplied, if your circumstances have changed, or if you think the decision is incorrect for any other reason. Write to the local Benefits Agency (social security) office, asking for your case to be reviewed and giving your reasons. If the request for a review is turned down, you can appeal against this decision.

Appeals

If you want to appeal fill in the appeal form at the back of leaflet NI 246 *How to Appeal*, which is available from Benefits Agency (social security) offices. The leaflet also tells you what happens when you appeal. You should send the appeal form back within three months of receiving the letter giving the decision. If you send the form back after three months, you should explain why your appeal was late. The chairperson of the tribunal will decide if the tribunal can hear your appeal, but a late appeal can be accepted only if certain strict conditions are met. When you complete the form, you should say which decision you wish to appeal against, and why you think the decision is wrong. Sometimes the adjudication officer may be able to change the decision on the basis of this information.

The tribunal

After writing your letter, you will be sent a copy of all the documents relevant to your case and you will be asked if you wish to attend an independent tribunal. If you do not write saying you wish to attend, your case will be dealt with based on the written information you and the adjudication officer provide. However, if possible you should try to attend a tribunal in person as this may give you a better opportunity to explain the position. At the tribunal hearing your case will be assessed by three people not connected with the DSS. There will also be an adjudication officer present.

When you arrive at the tribunal, a clerk will explain the procedures, which are intended to be as informal as possible. You will be given time to put your case and the tribunal will ask questions. The clerk should reimburse your travel expenses before you leave. The tribunal must decide whether the adjudication officer made the right decision according to the law, but cannot change a decision just because it seems unfair. You may be told the outcome straight away; otherwise notification of the decision will be sent to you later.

Secretary of State decisions

Certain decisions are made on behalf of the Secretary of State, such as the number of NI contributions you have made or how benefits are paid. If you disagree with this type of decision, you can ask for it to be reconsidered. You should write to the local Benefits Agency (social security) office giving the reasons why you disagree.

See social security leaflet NI 246 or the detailed guide NI 260.

OCCUPATIONAL AND PERSONAL PENSIONS

This section summarises how occupational and personal pensions can affect the State benefits you receive. It is not within the scope of this book to give information about the different types of pension scheme, but details are given on how to obtain further information or deal with problems.

How State benefits are affected

In general the State Pension and other benefits will not be affected by an occupational or personal pension. However, an occupational or personal pension will be counted as income in full for the purposes of benefits such as Income Support, income-based Jobseeker's Allowance (JSA), Housing Benefit and Council Tax Benefit. It can also reduce the amount of contribution-based JSA you get, as explained on page 23. If you receive a pension or benefit and wish to claim an increase for a dependent wife or husband, any occupational or personal pension they receive will be counted as earnings and may affect your increase, as explained on pages 4–5.

Getting advice

If you have a problem relating to an occupational or personal pension scheme that you cannot sort out with your employer or pension provider, you can contact the Pensions Advisory Service (OPAS, 11 Belgrave Road, London SW1V 1RB) or a Citizens Advice Bureau. OPAS is an independent voluntary organisation with a network of local advisers who can offer free help and advice. If OPAS cannot resolve your problem, they may suggest that you make a complaint to the Pensions Ombudsman, or to the Insurance Ombudsman Bureau in the case of a personal pension.

See Age Concern Books annual publication *The Pensions Handbook* for further information about different types of pension.

Income-Related (Means-Tested) Benefits

This part of Your Rights *describes benefits that older people may be able to claim depending on their income and savings. It covers Income Support, Housing Benefit and Council Tax Benefit, which help with regular weekly expenses, and the Social Fund, which provides lump-sum payments for exceptional expenses. Many older people do not claim the income-related benefits they are entitled to, so you should make sure that you are not losing out.*

Income-based Jobseeker's Allowance, which is paid to unemployed people under pension age, is not described, but it is calculated in a very similar way to Income Support.

INCOME SUPPORT (NOT TAXABLE)

This benefit helps with weekly basic living expenses by topping up your income to a level set by the Government. You do not need to have paid National Insurance (NI) contributions to qualify for Income Support, but your income and any savings and capital will be taken into account.

If you receive Income Support, you are also likely to qualify for Housing Benefit and/or Council Tax Benefit, which are based on similar rules. These benefits help with rent and Council Tax payments. If your income is too high for you to qualify for Income Support, you may still be entitled to Housing Benefit and Council Tax Benefit.

Income Support can be paid to home owners, tenants, and people in other circumstances such as living with family or friends. Once you get Income Support, you may also get other benefits such as a winter fuel payment (see p 99), free dental treatment (see pp 117–118) and possibly lump-sum payments from the Social Fund (see pp 48–52).

See social security guide IS 20 for detailed information.

Who qualifies?

You may receive Income Support if you fulfil all the following conditions:

- Your savings are £8,000 or less (£16,000 if you live in a residential or nursing home).
- You have a low income.
- You are aged 60 or over or you are under 60 but do not need to 'sign on' as unemployed, for example because you are ill or you are a carer. Unemployed people receive income-based Jobseeker's Allowance instead (see pp 22–24).
- You do not work 16 hours a week or more and your partner (if you have one) does not work 24 hours a week or more.

- You are habitually resident in the UK. If you have entered the UK within five years of your claim, you will be asked about this. The habitual residence test can apply to all claimants including British citizens. Other people in certain immigration categories may also be refused benefit. Contact a local advice agency if you need further advice.

A 'partner' is your husband or wife or someone of the opposite sex who you live with as though you were married. Throughout this section the word 'partner' will be used instead of 'spouse' because you do not have to be married to be treated as a couple. You apply for Income Support for yourself and your partner. If you live with someone else such as a friend, you can both apply for Income Support separately.

How to work it out

Income Support is worked out by using the following steps, which are explained below:

1 Add up the value of your savings, but note that certain types of savings are ignored.
2 Add up your weekly income, but note that certain kinds of income are ignored.
3 Work out the amount the Government says you need to live on, called the 'applicable amount'.
4 Compare your applicable amount with your income to see whether you are entitled to benefit.

1 Your savings

Throughout this book the term 'savings' is used to cover savings, capital, investments and property.

If your savings are more than £8,000, you cannot get Income Support. For a couple, savings are added together, but the limit is the same. Since April 1996, different savings limits have applied to people claiming Income Support in residential and nursing homes, as explained on pages 105–106.

If you have savings of between £3,000 and £8,000, an income of £1 a week for every £250 (or part of £250) over £3,000 will be taken into account when working out your benefit. For example, savings of £3,480 will be treated as an income of £2 a week; savings of £5,760 will be treated as £12 a week. This is called 'tariff income'. Savings of £3,000 or less will not affect your benefit.

- **If you 'deprive' yourself of savings in order to get benefit or to increase the amount of benefit, you will be considered as still having those savings. Depriving yourself of savings might include giving money to your family or buying expensive items in order to gain benefit. You should seek advice if you are refused benefit because of this.**

Savings and capital are normally valued at their current market or surrender value. If there are expenses involved in selling them, 10 per cent will be deducted. Most forms of savings and capital will be taken into account, including:

- cash;
- bank and building society accounts (including current accounts that do not pay interest);
- National Savings accounts and certificates (valued according to rules which the local Benefits Agency (social security) office will explain);
- premium bonds;
- stocks and shares;
- property;
- a share of any savings you own jointly with other people – these will be divided equally by the number of joint owners to calculate your share.

Some types of savings will be ignored, including:

- the value of your home if you own it and are living there;
- the surrender value of a life assurance policy (although if a policy is cashed in the money you receive will normally be counted);

- arrears of certain benefits such as Attendance Allowance, Disability Living Allowance or Income Support for 52 weeks from the date you receive them;
- your personal possessions, unless they have been bought in order to reduce your savings.

Your money should not normally be counted as both 'income' and 'savings'. So if, for example, your pension is paid four-weekly into a bank account, this should not be assessed as part of your savings unless it is still unspent at the end of the four-week period.

2 Your income

Income includes earnings, State benefits, occupational or personal pensions and any other money you have coming in after tax and NI contributions have been paid. For a couple, the income of both partners is added together when calculating Income Support.

However, some income may be fully or partly ignored when the Benefits Agency (social security) office works out your benefit.

Income that will be fully ignored includes:

- Housing Benefit and Council Tax Benefit;
- the mobility component of Disability Living Allowance;
- Attendance Allowance and the care component of Disability Living Allowance, although there are special rules for people in residential or nursing homes, as explained on pages 111–112;
- actual interest or income from savings or capital of £8,000 or less (only tariff income will be counted, as explained above). Interest is not counted as income but once it is paid into an account it will be counted as part of your savings;
- the special war widow's pension introduced in April 1990 for 'pre-1973 widows', which is now £54.70 (in addition to the £10 of a War Widow's Pension outlined below);
- payments made to you (for example by a relative or charity) for things not covered by benefit such as telephone costs,

TV rental or holidays, as long as you actually use them for these purposes.

The following are examples of parts of weekly income that will also be ignored:

- £5 of your earnings if you work part-time and are single;
- £10 of your or your partner's earnings from part-time work;
- £15 of earnings if you work part-time and you are a carer receiving the carer premium or in certain circumstances when you or your partner is disabled (instead of the £5 or £10 listed above);
- £10 of a War Widow's Pension or War Disablement Pension;
- £20 of regular payments from a friend, relative or charity, unless these are fully ignored, as described above (but this £20 will not be ignored on top of £10 from a war pension because the total amount from these two types of income that can be ignored must not be more than £20);
- £4 of any payment from a subtenant living in your home;
- £13.25 of any payment from a subtenant which includes an amount for heating;
- £20 income from a boarder plus half of the boarder's charge over £20.

Having decided what kinds of income will be ignored, add up the rest of your income, including tariff income for savings between £3,000 and £8,000. The total is the weekly income used to work out your Income Support.

3 Your applicable amount

This is the weekly amount intended to meet your day-to-day living needs. It is worked out by adding together the personal allowance for a single person or a couple and any premiums that apply to you. Premiums are awarded to particular groups such as those over certain ages and disabled people. For Income Support certain housing costs for home owners can also be included, as explained on pages 43–45. Allowances and premiums for children are not covered here. Once you have worked out your applicable amount, you will be able to check whether you are likely to qualify for one or more of the income-related benefits (Income Support, Housing Benefit and Council Tax Benefit).

Personal allowances

The personal allowances for people over 25 are shown below:

Single person   £50.35
Couple   £79.00

Premiums

These premiums are part of the system of income-related benefits. You must add these to your personal allowance to see if you qualify for Income Support, Housing Benefit and/or Council Tax Benefit. The six premiums described here are the ones that apply to people aged 60 or over, disabled people and carers. You can be awarded only one out of the following premiums: pensioner premium, enhanced pensioner premium, higher pensioner premium and disability premium.

If you fulfil the conditions for more than one of these, you will be awarded whichever is higher. However, the severe disability premium and the carer premium can be awarded in addition to other premiums.

Pensioner premium

If you are single and aged 60–74, you will get this premium (unless you qualify for the higher pensioner premium, described below). For a couple, you must both be under 75 and one or both of you must be 60 or over. The rates are:

Single person   £20.10
Couple   £30.35

Enhanced pensioner premium

This is awarded to single people aged 75–79 and to couples when one or both are 75–79 and both are under 80. The rates are:

Single person	£22.35
Couple	£33.55

Higher pensioner premium

You will get this if you are aged 80 or over or if you are aged 60-79 and fulfil the disability conditions for a disability premium (see below). For a couple, only one of you needs to fulfil either of these conditions. The rates are:

Single person	£27.20
Couple	£38.90

Disability premium

This is given to disabled people under 60. To be counted as 'disabled', you must normally be getting a disability benefit such as Attendance Allowance, Disability Living Allowance (any level or component), Severe Disablement Allowance or the long-term rate of Incapacity Benefit or be registered as blind. For a couple, only one of you needs to fulfil these conditions. The rates are:

Single person	£21.45
Couple	£30.60

People may also be able to receive the disability premium in some situations where they have been unable to work for at least 52 weeks but do not receive one of the disability benefits listed above. (You cannot qualify for the higher pensioner premium in this way.)

Severe disability premium

Single people will get this provided they 'live alone' (but see below for exceptions to this) and receive Attendance Allowance or the middle or highest level of the care component of Disability Living Allowance (DLA), with no one receiving Invalid Care Allowance for looking after them. However, there are exceptions to the living alone rule: for example, you can still get this premium if you live with someone who also gets Attendance Allowance (or the middle or highest level of the care component of DLA), or with someone who is registered blind, or with a paid helper supplied by a charity, or in some cases where you are a joint tenant or joint owner and share the housing costs. If you are not sure if you qualify, seek further advice as the rules can be complicated.

If you have a partner and you receive Attendance Allowance (or the middle or highest level of the care component of DLA), you can receive this premium if:

- your partner also gets Attendance Allowance (or the middle or highest level of the care component of DLA) or he or she is registered blind; *and*
- no one receives Invalid Care Allowance for looking after you; *and*
- you 'live alone' as described above.

If your partner also receives Attendance Allowance (or the middle or highest level of the care component of DLA) and neither of you has a carer receiving Invalid Care Allowance, you will receive the double rate. The rates are:

Single person	£38.50
Couple, one person qualifying	£38.50
Couple, both qualifying	£77.00

- **Remember that you can get this premium as well as either the disability or the higher pensioner premium.**

Carer premium

This premium is given to carers who are receiving Invalid Care Allowance (ICA – see pp 81–84). It will also be given to people who applied for ICA on or after 1 October 1990 and fulfil all the conditions but cannot receive it because they are getting another benefit instead.

For example, if you are receiving a Widow's Pension of £64.70, you will not be paid ICA as well. However, if you apply for ICA, you may receive a letter saying that you are entitled to ICA but cannot be paid it, which you can show to the Benefits Agency (social security) office (for Income Support) or the council (for Housing and Council Tax Benefit), who will award you the premium.

The carer premium continues to be paid for eight weeks after the person you care for dies, or you cease being a carer for some other reason. The rates for the carer premium are:

Single person	£13.65
Couple, one person qualifying	£13.65
Couple, both qualifying	£27.30

● **Warning: If the person you care for receives the severe disability premium (see above), they will lose this if you are awarded ICA. You might be able to receive an extra £13.65 a week through the carer premium while the person you care for would lose a premium worth £38.50. If you are not sure whether to claim ICA or not, get advice first.**

4 Calculating Income Support

Once you have worked out your applicable amount by adding together your personal allowance and any premiums, compare this figure with your income. If your income is less than your applicable amount, you will qualify for Income Support (depending on your savings). If your income is the same or more, you will not get Income Support but you may get Housing Benefit and/or Council Tax Benefit.

Example

Rose Williams is aged 76, and lives alone in a council flat. Her only income is the State Pension of £64.70 a week. She has savings of £950.

Rose adds up her income

Retirement Pension	£64.70

Rose works out her applicable amount

Personal allowance	£50.35
Enhanced pensioner premium	£22.35
Total	£72.70

Rose's income of £64.70 a week is less than her applicable amount of £72.70. The difference is £8.00. This is how much Income Support she will get on top of her Retirement Pension.

Rose will also get Housing Benefit and Council Tax Benefit to cover all her rent and Council Tax.

Example

Bill and Mary McConnell are a married couple both aged 70. Their joint State Pensions come to £103.40 and Bill gets a small pension of £20 a week from his old job. They live in their own home and they have savings of £3,800. Mary suffers with rheumatoid arthritis and gets Attendance Allowance.

Bill and Mary add up their income, ignoring Mary's Attendance Allowance

State Pension	£103.40
Work pension	£20.00
Weekly tariff income from savings	£4.00
Total	£127.40

Bill and Mary work out their applicable amount

Personal allowance	£79.00
Higher pensioner premium	£38.90
Total	£117.90

Their income is £9.50 a week more than their applicable amount, so they do not qualify for Income Support. But they should claim Council Tax Benefit to get help with their Council Tax payments.

Help with housing costs

In addition to your personal allowance and any premiums, your Income Support applicable amount can include an addition for certain housing costs. The help applies mainly to home owners as rent and service charges for tenants are covered by Housing Benefit. If the loan is for more than £100,000 or your housing costs are considered too high (taking into account your situation), the amount added to the applicable amount may be restricted. If you are receiving Income Support or have been receiving it within the last 26 weeks, you will be able to get help with the interest on a new loan only in certain circumstances. You should seek advice before taking out a loan. Subject to the above restrictions, if you are aged 60 or over the housing costs which can be included are:

- mortgage interest;
- interest on a loan for certain repairs or improvements;
- ground rent;
- certain service charges.

If you receive help with mortgage interest, this will be paid directly to your lender. The amount of help given towards interest is based on a standard interest rate. This may mean that you get either more or less than you actually have to pay.

If you are under 60, the help with housing costs may be restricted for up to nine months.

See social security leaflet IS 8 for detailed information.

Deductions for people living in your home

The help with housing costs may be reduced if there is someone else living in your home apart from your partner or a dependent child. This is because people such as grown-up sons and daughters (sometimes called 'non-dependants') are expected to contribute to housing costs. However, no reduction will be made if you or your partner is blind or you or your partner receives Attendance Allowance or the care component of Disability Living Allowance.

The deductions made will depend on the circumstances of the person living with you. If he or she is aged 18 or over, works 16 hours a week or more, and has an income of at least £78 a week, there are the following rates:

Gross income of non-dependant	Weekly deduction
£78.00 to £115.99	£16.00
£116.00 to £151.99	£22.00
£152.00 to £199.99	£36.00
£200.00 to £249.00	£41.00
£250.00 or more	£45.00

For others aged 18 or over, or people aged 25 or over on Income Support or income-based Jobseeker's Allowance (JSA), the deduction will be £7; there is no deduction if the non-dependant is under 25 and receiving Income Support or income-based JSA. If there is a couple living with you, only one deduction will be made.

Example

Desmond and Marie Wilson (both aged 65) have a mortgage. Their mortgage interest is assessed as £30 a week, so their applicable amount is worked out in the following way:

Personal allowance for a couple	£79.00
Pensioner premium	£30.35
Weekly mortgage interest	£30.00
Total	£139.35

Their daughter who is 20 and earns £140 a week comes to live with them. There will therefore be a deduction of £22 from the amount allowed for mortgage interest. Their total Income Support applicable amount will then be reduced to £117.35. This means that, depending on their savings, Desmond and Marie will receive Income Support if their income is less than £117.35 a week.

Income Support for people in different circumstances

Living in someone else's home

If you live in someone else's home as a member of their household – for example, with your son or daughter – Income Support will be worked out in the normal way. However, if your son or daughter gets help with housing costs through Income Support, income-based JSA, Housing Benefit or Council Tax Benefit, this may be reduced because you are living there.

Boarders and hostel dwellers

If you are living in a hotel, guest house or hostel, or in board and lodgings, Income Support will be worked out in the normal way. You can claim Housing Benefit towards the rental element of your charges and some services. You will have to pay for meals, fuel and other items that are not covered by Housing Benefit from your weekly Income Support.

If you go into hospital

Income Support is reduced after six weeks if either you or your partner goes into hospital. If you are single, the personal allowance will be reduced to £16.20. You will not get any premiums, but you will still get housing costs. If you have a partner, you will get the normal amount minus £12.95.

After 52 weeks in hospital, a single person will have an applicable amount of £12.95 but no housing costs. If you have a partner, your personal allowance will be £12.95 and he or she will be assessed separately.

Residential and nursing homes

Income Support for people in residential or nursing homes is described on pages 105–106 and 109–111.

How to claim Income Support

You will need a claim form from the local Benefits Agency (social security) office. You can obtain this by calling in, writing, telephoning or sending in the tear-off slip from form IS 1, which you can get at the local Benefits Agency (social security) office or post office. If you need help with filling in the claim form, ask at the Benefits Agency, a Citizens Advice Bureau or a welfare rights advice agency.

At the time of writing a claim for Income Support can be backdated for up to three months in certain specified circumstances. However, the Government intends to restrict the time that benefit can be backdated to one month. As with the current rules, you will only get backdated benefit if there are special reasons or circumstances why you did not apply sooner. This change is expected to come into effect in June 1998. Once you are receiving Income Support you should let the Benefits Agency know of any changes in your circumstances that might affect your benefit.

Income Support and the Retirement Pension are normally paid together. If you collect your pension weekly at the post office, your Income Support will be paid with the pension. If you prefer, you can choose to have your Income Support and Retirement Pension paid weekly directly into a bank or building society account.

If you disagree with a decision

If you disagree with a decision that has been made about your Income Support (for example you may have been refused a premium), you can ask for the case to be reviewed or appeal against the decision (see pp 28–30). You also have the right to ask for more detailed information about why a decision was made.

THE SOCIAL FUND

The Social Fund provides lump-sum payments to people with low incomes in order to meet exceptional expenses. There are Funeral Payments, as described below, and Cold Weather Payments, which are explained on page 99. If you have other expenses, you may get help from the discretionary Social Fund in the form of Community Care Grants, Budgeting Loans or Crisis Loans.

The £1,000 capital limit for Social Fund payments described here applies only to people aged 60 or over. For younger people, a capital limit of £500 applies.

Funeral Payments

If you are responsible for the cost of a funeral and you or your partner is receiving Income Support, Housing Benefit, Council Tax Benefit, income-based Jobseeker's Allowance or Disability Working Allowance, you may be able to get a Funeral Payment to help towards the cost from the Social Fund. However, as explained below, there are restrictions on who can receive a payment and limits on the amount of the payment so it is important to check what you are entitled to before making the arrangements.

To receive a payment you should be the partner or close relative of the person who has died, or someone else who it is reasonable to expect to take responsibility for arranging the funeral. The person who died must have been resident in the UK and usually the funeral must take place in the UK.

However, unless you are the partner of the person who has died, the Benefits Agency may decide that it was not reasonable for you to have taken responsibility for the funeral costs. There may, for example, be another close relative who is not receiving a qualifying benefit or who has more savings than you.

The payment can cover reasonable burial and cremation costs plus up to £600 for other funeral expenses.

If you are entitled to a payment, any savings over £1,000 (£500 if you are under 60) will be taken into account, as will any money from the estate of the person who has died or money from insurance policies or pre-paid funeral plans. For example, if you have £1,300, you will be expected to put the first £300 towards the funeral, and you may then get help with the rest up to the maximum limit.

To make a claim you will need form SF 200 from your local Benefits Agency (social security) office. You normally have to claim within three months of the funeral, but the Government intends to reduce this time limit to one month from June 1998. It is advisable to check what you are entitled to before arranging a funeral.

See social security leaflet D 49 for what to do after a death.

The discretionary Social Fund

The payments described below are different from most other social security benefits in that they are discretionary, and Budgeting Loans and Crisis Loans have to be repaid. There is a limited budget for the discretionary Social Fund which restricts the overall amount that can be awarded in grants and loans in any financial year. There is a legal framework for the system and Social Fund Officers have to follow directions and take account of guidance which helps them make decisions. They must consider the circumstances of the people who apply and decide which applications can be met from the budget.

Community Care Grants

These are available to people on Income Support or income-based Jobseeker's Allowance and to people who are likely to receive these benefits on discharge from care within six weeks' time. The grants do not have to be repaid. Savings over £1,000 (£500 for people under 60) will be deducted from any grant awarded. For example, if you have £1,100 savings and you need an item costing £300 you would only receive a grant for

£200. If you are not sure whether you will get help, you have nothing to lose by applying. It is important to include all the relevant information (see below on 'How to apply').

The following grants are available:

- help with moving out of institutional or residential care (eg for a bed, a cooker, fuel connection or removal costs);
- help to enable you to remain living at home (eg for minor house repairs, bedding and essential furniture, removal costs to more suitable accommodation);
- help with exceptional pressures on families (eg caused by disability, chronic sickness or a breakdown in a relationship); *and*
- help with certain travel expenses (eg for visiting someone who is ill or attending a relative's funeral).

Budgeting Loans

These are available to people who have been on Income Support or income-based Jobseeker's Allowance for at least 26 weeks and need important items they cannot afford. The loans, which are interest-free, have to be repaid, and any savings over £1,000 (£500 for people under 60) will reduce the amount of the loan.

Items you may get a loan for include: costs of an essential move to more suitable accommodation, redecoration costs, clothing or furniture. You will be more likely to get a loan for something essential which is considered a high priority such as bedding than for an item with a lower priority.

Changes are planned to Budgeting Loans. These changes are expected to come into force in April 1999. For more information contact Age Concern England at the address on page 138.

Crisis Loans

These interest-free loans are available to anyone (not just people on Income Support or income-based Jobseeker's

Allowance) who needs money urgently in an emergency or as a result of a disaster (eg fire or flood). The Social Fund Officer will take into account any family savings or income which is available to you. You may be able to get a loan provided that this is the only way of preventing serious damage or risk to your health or safety or that of a member of your family.

Repayment of loans

Budgeting or Crisis Loans will be awarded only if the officer thinks you will be able to repay them. Normally repayments will be deducted from your benefit over a period of 78 weeks. In special circumstances the repayment period will be extended to 104 weeks.

The repayment rates will be fixed after taking into account your income and your existing and future commitments. In the case of Crisis Loans, repayments will not normally begin until after the period of crisis is over.

How to apply

To apply for a Community Care Grant or Budgeting Loan, you need application form SF 300 from your local Benefits Agency (social security) office. If you need a Crisis Loan, ask at the office.

You should give as much information as possible about your circumstances and why you need help (eg health problems). If there is not enough room on the form, use a separate sheet.

A welfare rights agency or Citizens Advice Bureau may be able to help you with the application. You may also wish to include a letter of support from your GP or social worker.

If you are unhappy about a decision

Community Care Grants and loans from the Social Fund are discretionary payments. If you disagree with a decision, you cannot appeal to a Social Security Appeal Tribunal, but instead there is a special system of review. The first stage of review is at the local office, and you are given the chance to put your case personally to a Social Fund officer. If you are still dissatisfied, you can take your case to a Social Fund inspector, who is independent of your local Benefits Agency.

For the other payments from the Social Fund – Funeral and Cold Weather Payments – there is a right of appeal to a Social Security Appeal Tribunal.

See social security leaflet SFL 2 or detailed guide SB 16 for more information about the Social Fund.

HOUSING BENEFIT AND COUNCIL TAX BENEFIT (NOT TAXABLE)

Housing Benefit provides help with rent, with certain service charges and, in Northern Ireland, with general rates. People who live in Northern Ireland and require information about rate rebates should contact Age Concern Northern Ireland.

Council Tax Benefit is a social security benefit which provides help with paying the Council Tax. See also 'Help with the Council Tax' on pages 113–114, which gives information about other ways your Council Tax bill may be reduced which are not related to your income or savings.

You may get Housing Benefit or Council Tax Benefit if you have a low income and your savings are no more than £16,000. You must also be 'habitually resident' in the UK, as mentioned on page 35. If you have a partner (that is, you are married or live with someone of the opposite sex as though you were married), the amount of benefit you get will be worked out on your combined savings and income.

Who qualifies for Housing Benefit?

You may get Housing Benefit if you are responsible for paying rent and you fulfil the conditions outlined above. Benefit is available to council, housing association and private tenants and to people in the following circumstances:

Boarders and people living in hostels may get Housing Benefit for the accommodation part of their charges and may also get Income Support or income-based Jobseeker's Allowance (see p 46).

People in private residential or nursing homes will not normally be able to receive Housing Benefit towards the home's fees, but see pages 112–113 for exceptions.

People living in a houseboat may get benefit for the mooring charges even if they own the houseboat.

People living in a caravan or mobile home may get help with the site charges even if they own the caravan or mobile home.

Joint tenants may receive Housing Benefit towards the part of the costs for which they are responsible.

People living with a landlord who is a close relative may claim Housing Benefit if they live separately in self-contained accommodation. However, they cannot claim benefit if they are part of the same household, or if it is not a 'commercial arrangement'. Get advice if you are unsure about your position.

Who qualifies for Council Tax Benefit?

There are two types of Council Tax Benefit – 'main Council Tax Benefit' and 'second adult rebate'. If you are responsible for paying the Council Tax, you may be able to receive main Council Tax Benefit provided that you fulfil the conditions outlined above. If you are jointly responsible for a bill with someone other than your partner, you can apply for help with your share of the tax.

The second adult rebate may be available to some people, regardless of their income and savings, who have one or more people with low incomes living with them. This is covered on pages 63–64, while the rest of this section covers the main benefit scheme.

How to work out your benefit

Housing Benefit and Council Tax Benefit are worked out using similar calculations. The rules outlined below apply to both benefits unless stated otherwise. To work out how much benefit you will get, follow the steps listed, which are then explained.

1 Calculate the maximum weekly rent and Council Tax for which you can get benefit.
2 Deduct an amount for non-dependants living in your home.
3 Add up the value of your savings, but note that certain types of savings are ignored.
4 Add up your weekly income, but note that certain kinds of income are ignored.
5 Work out the amount the Government says you need to live on, called the 'applicable amount'.
6 Calculate your benefit according to the formula explained below.
7 For Housing Benefit, check that the benefit is above the minimum amount payable, which is 50p a week. There is no minimum payment for Council Tax Benefit.

I Your rent and Council Tax

For Housing Benefit purposes, rent is the payment made to occupy your home. It also covers certain service charges – for example for furniture, cleaning communal areas, cleaning your rooms (if neither you nor your partner can do this), portering, entry phones, wardens and caretakers, rubbish removal. Also included in service charges is the cost of an emergency alarm system, but only if it has been installed in accommodation specially designed or adapted for older people or those with disabilities. At the time of writing, benefit for service charges is being reviewed so the rules may change. Contact Age Concern England for more information at the address on page 138.

You cannot get benefit for water rates and sewerage charges. Home owners cannot get Housing Benefit; however, they may get help with certain costs such as service charges and mortgage payments from Income Support or income-based Jobseeker's Allowance (see pp 43–45).

The maximum Housing Benefit you can get is 100 per cent of your rent including the service charges described above. However, the level of rent on which benefit is calculated may be reduced, as explained below.

High rents

If the local authority considers that your rent is too high or your accommodation is larger than you need (taking into account your circumstances) or that the rent has increased unreasonably while you have been getting Housing Benefit, it may restrict the amount of Housing Benefit.

In addition, some private tenants may face further benefit restrictions if their rent is higher than the typical rent for similar accommodation in the area. These restrictions will not apply to people who were already receiving benefit before 2 January 1996 and have not moved since. Occasionally these rules might also apply to housing association tenants. Before taking up a tenancy, you can ask the local authority for a 'pre-tenancy determination', which will tell you how much of the rent would be eligible for Housing Benefit. If restricting the amount of your rent that is eligible for benefit would cause you 'exceptional hardship', the local authority has some discretion to pay more benefit.

If you want to challenge a decision about your benefit or to ask the local authority to use its discretion, it is a good idea to get advice from a local agency. The rules on rent restrictions are complicated and are only covered briefly here. If you need more information, contact Age Concern or consult a book such as the *National Welfare Benefits Handbook* (see 'Further reading').

Council Tax

The maximum Council Tax Benefit you can get is 100 per cent of your bill. However, from April 1998 there are restrictions to the maximum amount of benefit for people in band F-H properties. If your property is in one of these bands your benefit will only be calculated on the basis of the level of council tax for a band E property in your area.

The benefit is based on the amount you are asked to pay after any 'discounts' or 'reductions' (see pp 113–114) have been given. For example, if you live alone you will receive a 25 per cent discount on your bill, and your benefit will be worked out after this has been deducted.

● Note that the calculations in this section are all done on a weekly basis. So if you pay your Council Tax in ten monthly instalments, you will first have to work out how much this would be per week over the whole year.

Heating charges

Some people have a charge for heating included in their rent. You cannot get Housing Benefit for heating and other fuel charges. If, for example, you pay £35 a week rent and £5 of that is for heating, you will only get a maximum of £30 Housing Benefit, as the charge for fuel will be deducted.

If your weekly fuel charges are not stated as a separate amount, the council will deduct the amounts listed below:

Heating	£9.25
Hot water	£1.15
Cooking	£1.15
Lighting	£0.80
All fuel	£12.35

The amounts are lower if you occupy only one room.

2 Deductions for non-dependants living in your home

A deduction will normally be made from both your Housing Benefit and your Council Tax Benefit if you have someone else living with you who is not your partner or a dependent child nor a joint tenant or joint owner. This is because people such as grown-up sons and daughters (called 'non-dependants') are expected to contribute to housing costs. However, no deduction will be made if you or your partner is blind or receives Attendance Allowance or the care component of Disability Living Allowance. There are also some types of non-dependant who do not give rise to a deduction – for example, students or people in hospital for more than six weeks.

If the person living with you is aged 18 or over, works 16 hours a week or more, and has a gross income of at least £78 a week, the rates of deduction are as follows:

Gross income of non-dependant	Weekly deduction from rent	Weekly deduction from Council Tax
£78.00 to £115.99	£16.00	£2.00
£116.00 to £151.99	£22.00	£4.00
£152.00 to £199.99	£36.00	£4.00
£200.00 to £249.99	£41.00	£5.00
£250 or more	£45.00	£6.00

If the person who lives with you receives Income Support or income-based Jobseeker's Allowance (JSA), there will be no deduction from your Housing Benefit if they are under 25 and a £7 deduction if they are aged 25 or over. There will be a £7 deduction from your Housing Benefit for anyone else who is aged 18 or over and does not fall into any of the categories already mentioned.

For Council Tax Benefit there is no deduction for a non-dependant receiving Income Support or income-based JSA while for others aged 18 or over not covered above there will be a £2.00 deduction.

Only one deduction is made for a non-dependent couple living with you.

3 Your savings

Throughout this book the term 'savings' is used to cover savings, capital, investments and property.

If your savings are more than £16,000, you cannot get Housing Benefit or Council Tax Benefit. For a couple, savings are added together, but the limit is the same.

If you have savings of between £3,000 and £16,000, an income of £1 a week for every £250 (or part of £250) over £3,000 will be taken into account in working out your benefit. For example, savings of £3,480 will be treated as an income of £2 a week. Savings of £10,760 will be treated as £32 a week. This is called 'tariff income'. Savings of £3,000 or less will not affect your benefit.

● **If you 'deprive' yourself of savings in order to get benefit or to increase the amount of benefit, you will be considered as still having those savings. Depriving yourself of savings might include giving money away to your family or buying expensive items in order to gain benefit. You should seek advice if you are refused benefit because of this.**

Savings and capital are normally valued at their current market or surrender value. If there are expenses involved in selling them, 10 per cent will be deducted. Most forms of savings and capital will be taken into account, including:

● cash;
● bank and building society accounts (including current accounts that do not pay interest);
● National Savings accounts and certificates (valued according to rules which the local authority will explain);
● premium bonds;
● stocks and shares;
● property;
● a share of any savings you own jointly with other people – these will be divided equally by the number of joint owners to calculate your share.

Some types of savings and capital will be ignored, including:

- the value of your home if you own it and are living there;
- the surrender value of a life assurance policy (although if a policy is cashed in the money you receive will normally be counted);
- arrears of certain benefits such as Attendance Allowance, DLA or Income Support for 52 weeks from the date you receive them;
- your personal possessions, unless they have been bought in order to reduce your savings.

Your money should not normally be counted as both 'income' and 'savings'. So if, for example, your pension is paid four-weekly into a bank account, this should not be assessed as part of your savings unless it is still unspent at the end of the four-week period.

4 Your income

Income includes earnings, State benefits, occupational or personal pensions and any other money you have coming in after tax and NI contributions have been paid. For a couple, the income of both partners is added together when calculating benefit.

However, some income may be fully or partly ignored when your benefit is calculated. Income that will be fully ignored includes:

- Income Support;
- Disability Living Allowance;
- Attendance Allowance;
- actual interest or income from savings or capital of £16,000 or less (only tariff income will be counted, as explained above). Interest is not counted as income but once it is paid into an account it will be counted as part of your savings;
- the special war widow's pension introduced in April 1990 for 'pre-1973 widows', which is now £54.70 (in addition to the £10 of a War Widow's Pension outlined below);
- payments made to you (for example by a relative or charity) for things not covered by benefit such as telephone costs,

TV rental or holidays, as long as you actually use them for these purposes.

The following are examples of parts of weekly income that will also be ignored:

- £5 of your earnings if you work part-time and are single;
- £10 of your or your partner's earnings from part-time work;
- £15 of earnings if you work part-time and you are a carer receiving the carer premium or in certain circumstances when you or your partner is disabled (instead of the £5 or £10 listed above);
- £10 of a War Widow's Pension or War Disablement Pension (the local authority has the discretion to increase the amount from these pensions that is ignored when working out your benefit, but not all authorities operate such schemes);
- £20 of regular payments from a friend, relative or charity, unless these are fully ignored, as described above (but this £20 will not be ignored on top of £10 from a war pension because the total amount from these two types of income that can be ignored must not be more than £20);
- £4 of any payment from a subtenant living in your home;
- £13.25 of any payment from a subtenant which includes an amount for heating;
- £20 income from a boarder plus half of the boarder's charge over £20.

To work out your benefit, decide what kinds of income will be ignored and add up the remainder (including tariff income for savings between £3,000 and £16,000).

5 Your applicable amount

This is the weekly amount intended to meet your day-to-day living needs. If your income is higher than this, you may still get some help with rent and the Council Tax.

Your applicable amount for Housing Benefit and Council Tax Benefit is worked out in the same way as for Income Support except that there are no additions for the housing costs of home owners. To work out your applicable amount, add up the personal allowance and any premiums that apply to you (see pp 38–42).

6 Calculating Housing Benefit and Council Tax Benefit

Once you have worked out your applicable amount, compare this figure with your income, including any tariff income from savings over £3,000. If your income is the same as or less than your applicable amount, you will normally get all your rent and Council Tax paid (unless, for example, there are deductions for ineligible service charges, for other people living in your home or because your rent or Council Tax band is considered too high).

If your income is more than your applicable amount, the maximum benefit you can get is reduced. You first work out the difference between your income and your applicable amount. The maximum Housing Benefit payable is reduced by 65 per cent of this difference. The maximum Council Tax Benefit is reduced by 20 per cent of the difference.

Another way of explaining the calculation is to say that your maximum Housing Benefit is reduced by 65p for every pound that your income is more than your applicable amount. Your maximum Council Tax Benefit is reduced by 20p for every pound that your income is more than your applicable amount.

Example

Julie Walker is aged 64 and lives alone. Her income consists of a State Pension (Basic and Additional Pension) of £75 a week and the mobility component of Disability Living Allowance of £35.85 a week. She has £500 savings and pays £40 a week rent and £6 a week Council Tax.

The maximum Housing Benefit she can get is £40 a week (100 per cent of her rent). The maximum Council Tax Benefit she can get is £6 a week (100 per cent of her Council Tax). There are no non-dependant deductions because she lives alone.

Her savings will not affect her benefit, and the total amount of her income counted will be £75 because her Disability Living Allowance is ignored.

Julie's applicable amount is set out below

Personal allowance	£50.35
Higher pensioner premium	£27.20
Total	£77.55

Her income is less than her applicable amount, so she will get the maximum Housing Benefit of £40 a week for rent and the maximum Council Tax Benefit of £6 a week. She will also qualify for Income Support and should make a claim.

Example

Nimesh and Anila Khan are both aged 68 and live in a rented house. They pay £58 a week rent which includes £8 heating. Their Council Tax is £9 a week. They have a State Pension of £103.40 a week, Nimesh's occupational pension of £23.95 a week, and savings of £3,400.

The maximum Housing Benefit they can get is £50 (£58 minus the heating charge of £8). The maximum Council Tax Benefit they can get is £9. They have nobody else living with them so there will be no non-dependant deductions.

Nimesh and Anila add up their income

State Pension	£103.40
Occupational pension	£23.95
Tariff income (for savings over £3,000)	£2.00
Total	£129.35

They calculate their applicable amount

Personal allowance	£79.00
Pensioner premium	£30.35
Total	£109.35

Their income is more than their applicable amount, the difference being £20 (£129.35 – £109.35).

Their weekly benefit is worked out in the following way

Rent

100% of rent	£50.00
Less 65% of difference	
(65% of £20)	£13.00
Housing Benefit	£37.00

Council Tax

100% of tax	£9.00
Less 20% of difference	
(20% of £20)	£4.00
Council Tax Benefit	£5.00

Total benefit is

Housing Benefit	£37.00
Council Tax Benefit	£5.00

Nimesh and Anila will have to pay £13 a week for rent plus the £8 heating charge and £4 towards the Council Tax.

If their daughter, who is 20, works full-time and earns £160 a week, comes to live with them their Housing Benefit will be reduced by £36 and their Council Tax Benefit by £4 a week. They would therefore get just £1 a week Housing Benefit and £1 a week Council Tax Benefit.

Second adult rebate

If you are solely liable to pay the Council Tax, you might get a second adult rebate if one or more people with a low income live with you, regardless of the level of your savings and income. This will usually apply only to people who do not have a partner. You may get a 25 per cent rebate if you are responsible for the Council Tax and you have one or more people receiving Income Support or income-based Jobseeker's

Allowance (JSA) living with you. A 15 per cent rebate is given if the person or people living with you have a joint gross income of less than £116; there is a 7.5 per cent rebate if their income is between £116 and £151.99. In assessing the income of people living with you, no account is taken of Attendance Allowance, Disability Living Allowance or the income of anyone receiving Income Support or income-based JSA.

Example

Janice Grant is a widow who owns her own home. Her son is living with her and receives income-based JSA. Her Council Tax bill for the year is £400. She is not entitled to the main Council Tax Benefit because she has £18,000 savings. However, she applies for a rebate and receives the second adult rebate of 25 per cent (£100) because her son receives income-based JSA.

Some people will be entitled to the main Council Tax Benefit and the second adult rebate. In this case the local authority will award you whichever benefit will give you the greater amount.

Only brief details have been given here as this system can be complicated, so contact your local authority or advice agency if you need further information.

Benefit for people in different circumstances

Absence from home

If you go into hospital on a temporary basis, you can continue to get Housing Benefit and Council Tax Benefit for up to one year. However, the amount you receive may be reduced after six weeks. If you are temporarily away from home for other reasons, benefit will be paid for up to 13 weeks or up to 52 weeks depending on the reason for your absence. Contact the local authority or local advice agency if you need more information about this. You cannot get benefit if you sub-let your home while you are away.

Benefit for two homes

You can normally only get Housing Benefit for one home. However, if you have moved to a new home and payments on both homes are *unavoidable*, you may get benefit on both for up to four weeks. There are, however, only certain specific circumstances when payments are made for two homes, so ask the local authority whether you qualify.

Council Tax Benefit is payable only for the home in which you are resident. It is not payable for second homes.

Hardship relief

In cases of hardship, the local authority has the discretion to increase the amount of benefit you can receive if your circumstances are 'exceptional'. They could increase the amount of Housing Benefit and Council Tax Benefit you get up to the maximum amounts. You should ask if you think you should be treated as a special case.

How to claim

If you are claiming Income Support or income-based Jobseeker's Allowance, you will also be given claim forms for Housing Benefit and Council Tax Benefit. After any entitlement to Income Support or income-based JSA has been worked out, the local authority will be notified so that they can calculate your Housing Benefit and Council Tax Benefit. If you are a private or housing association tenant, the local authority will send you a form to complete, asking for details of your accommodation and the rent you pay.

If you are not claiming Income Support or income-based JSA, you claim Housing Benefit and Council Tax Benefit directly from your local authority.

If you are a couple, only one of you should claim for benefit – it does not matter if the bill is sent in joint names or just to one of you. Your benefit will be calculated on the basis of your combined income and savings.

Before the local authority can work out how much to pay, they may require evidence of your income, savings and the amount of rent you pay. Benefit is normally awarded for a fixed period of up to 60 weeks, and you will receive another claim form to make a fresh claim at the end of this period.

At the time of writing the local authority can backdate your claim for benefit for up to 52 weeks if you can show that you had a good reason for claiming late. However it is the Government's intention that from October 1998 you will only receive up to one month's backdating and this may only apply in certain specified circumstances. You should let the local authority know about any changes in your circumstances that might affect your benefit.

If the local authority delays your claim

The local authority should let you know within 14 days of your claim whether you qualify for help as long as you have provided any information and evidence needed. However, this sometimes takes much longer. If you should suffer hardship because the local authority has not yet worked out your claim for benefit, contact your nearest Citizens Advice Bureau or advice centre for help. If pressure from them cannot speed up the assessment, it may be necessary to ask a local councillor to take the matter up or refer your complaint to the Local Government Ombudsman, who investigates maladministration.

How it is paid

For council tenants, Housing Benefit is usually paid by reducing the rent. If you are a private or housing association tenant, your Housing Benefit may be paid to you by cheque or into a bank account or direct to your landlord.

Most people will pay the Council Tax direct to their local authority, so when you claim benefit your bill will be reduced accordingly. Where this is not possible because, for example, you have already paid the whole bill, the local authority may send you a refund.

Overpayment

If you are paid too much benefit, this is known as an overpayment and in most circumstances the council can ask you to repay this money. However, an overpayment cannot normally be recovered if it was caused by an 'official error' and you could not reasonably be expected to have known you were being overpaid at the time. Even if the local authority can recover the benefit, it does have some discretion about whether to do so. It is a good idea to seek further advice if you are being asked to repay benefit.

If you disagree with a decision

You can write to the local authority at any time, asking for further information about how decisions about your benefit have been made. You can also ask for a review of a decision relating to your benefit, perhaps because you think you have been awarded the wrong amount.

You should write to the local authority explaining why you would like the decision reviewed. You should do this within six weeks of when the local authority sent the decision, although the local authority may extend this time limit if there are good reasons why you have not written sooner. You must sign the letter yourself. The local authority will then write to you to change the decision or to tell you why it has not changed it.

Appealing to a review board

If you still disagree with a decision, you can ask for a further review, but you must ask for it in writing giving the reasons why you think the local authority's decision is wrong. You must sign the letter yourself. You should write within 28 days of the decision on the first review, although this time limit may be extended if there are good reasons why you have not written sooner. Your case will then go to a review board, which consists of at least three local councillors. You can attend the hearing and put your case or a representative can do this on your behalf. The board's decision must normally be sent to you within seven days, with the reasons for the decision.

If you appeal to a review board, get advice from a Citizens Advice Bureau, welfare rights advice centre or independent housing advice centre. They may be able to find someone who can represent you at the hearing.

Benefits for People with Disabilities and Their Carers

This part of Your Rights *describes the main benefits available to people with disabilities and those who look after them.*

Disability Living Allowance and Attendance Allowance are intended to help with the extra costs associated with disability while other benefits such as Incapacity Benefit and Severe Disablement Allowance are paid to people who are unable to work or can work only to a limited extent because of their disability.

ATTENDANCE ALLOWANCE AND DISABILITY LIVING ALLOWANCE (NOT TAXABLE)

Attendance Allowance and Disability Living Allowance are intended to help with the costs of illness or disability. Which one you claim depends on your age when you become ill or disabled and your age when you make your claim.

To qualify for Disability Living Allowance (DLA) you must have become ill or disabled before the age of 65 and you must claim before your 65th birthday. If you cannot claim DLA because you are 65 or over, you should claim Attendance Allowance instead.

This section covers first the conditions for Attendance Allowance and then the conditions for Disability Living Allowance; the third part gives information that applies to both allowances.

Attendance Allowance

This is a benefit for people who need help with personal care, or need supervision, or need someone to watch over them because of physical or mental illness or disability. It does not depend on National Insurance (NI) contributions, is not affected by savings or income, and will not normally affect or be affected by other benefits or pensions received.

However, Attendance Allowance is normally counted as income if you are receiving Income Support in a residential or nursing home, as explained on pages 111–112.

There are two weekly rates:

Higher rate	£51.30
Lower rate	£34.30

Who qualifies for Attendance Allowance?

To qualify for Attendance Allowance you must fulfil all the following conditions:

- You are aged 65 or older.
- You meet the day and/or night conditions described below.
- You must also normally have satisfied the disability conditions for at least six months, but there are 'special rules' for people who are terminally ill, as explained on page 79.
- You are normally resident in the UK when you make your claim, and (unless you are applying under the special rules for terminally ill people) have been here for at least 26 weeks of the last 12 months.

You will receive the lower rate if you fulfil either the day or the night conditions. You will get the higher rate if you fulfil both day and night conditions.

You can receive the allowance if you live alone or with other people and regardless of whether or not you receive any help from someone else – what matters is that you need help with personal care, supervision or watching over, not whether you are actually getting help. You do not have to spend the allowance on paying for care: it is up to you how you use it. However, your local authority may take it into account when assessing whether, and how much, you need to pay for any social services you have.

Day conditions

You can get the allowance if you are so disabled that you require frequent help throughout the day with your normal 'bodily functions' such as eating, getting up or down stairs, going to the toilet or washing. 'Seeing' is considered a bodily function – so, for example, if you are visually impaired and need guidance when walking or someone to read your mail, this could help you satisfy the requirement for needing 'frequent help'. A test case in 1997 ruled that help needed with social activities can be taken into account. You can also get the allowance if you need continual supervision throughout the day to avoid putting yourself or others in substantial danger.

Night conditions

You can get the allowance if you are so disabled that you require prolonged (periods of at least 20 minutes) or repeated (at least twice nightly) attention during the night to help you with your bodily functions – for example, going to the toilet and getting in and out of bed. You can also get the allowance if another person needs to be awake for a prolonged period or at frequent intervals throughout the night in order to watch over you to avoid putting yourself or others in substantial danger.

The next section covers the qualifying conditions for Disability Living Allowance. You should turn to pages 76–81 for information that covers both allowances such as how to make a claim and what happens if you are away from home.

Disability Living Allowance

This benefit replaced Attendance Allowance and Mobility Allowance for people who become ill or disabled before the age of 65. It is for disabled people who:

- need help with personal care, or need supervision, or need someone to watch over them; or
- are unable to walk, have great difficulty walking, or need someone with them when walking outdoors; or
- need help with both of these.

Disability Living Allowance (DLA) does not depend on NI contributions, is not affected by savings or income, and will not normally affect other benefits or pensions received. However, the care component of DLA is normally counted as income if you are receiving Income Support in a residential or nursing home, as explained on pages 111–112.

There are two parts to DLA: the 'care component', which is paid at one of three rates, and the 'mobility component', which has two different levels. The weekly rates are:

DLA care component		DLA mobility component	
Highest rate	£51.30	Higher rate	£35.85
Middle rate	£34.30	Lower rate	£13.60
Lowest rate	£13.60		

Who qualifies for DLA?

To qualify for DLA you must fulfil the following conditions:

- You meet one or more of the care or mobility conditions described below.
- You are aged under 65.
- You must also normally have satisfied the disability conditions for at least three months, and be expected to satisfy them for at least the next six months, but there are 'special rules' for people who are terminally ill, as explained on page 79.
- You are normally resident in the UK when you make your claim, and (unless you are applying under the special rules for terminally ill people) have been here for at least 26 weeks of the last 12 months.

Although you must have become disabled, and made a claim, before the age of 65, once you are awarded the allowance it will continue, without an age limit, as long as you satisfy either the care or the mobility conditions.

The care component

The care component of DLA is for people who need help with personal care, supervision or watching over because of physical or mental illness or disability. It does not matter if you live alone or with other people, or whether or not you receive any help from someone else – what matters is that you need help with personal care, supervision or watching over, not whether you are actually getting help. You do not have to spend the allowance on paying for care: it is up to you how you use it. However, your local authority may take it into account when assessing whether, and how much, you need to pay for any social services you have.

You will receive £13.60 if you fulfil the lower-rate conditions but not the day or night conditions described below. You will receive the middle level if you fulfil either the day or the night conditions while the highest level is for those who fulfil both day and night conditions. You will see that the day and night conditions are the same as those for Attendance Allowance.

Lower-rate conditions

You will fulfil this condition if you need help with 'bodily functions' for a significant portion of the day, either at one single period or a number of times. For example, you might need some help to get up in the morning and go to bed in the evening but manage alone for the rest of the day. You will also fulfil this condition if you could not prepare a main cooked meal for yourself even if you had the ingredients.

Day conditions

You will fulfil this condition if you are so disabled that you require frequent help throughout the day with your normal bodily functions such as eating, getting up or down stairs, going to the toilet or washing. 'Seeing' is considered a bodily function – so, for example, if you are visually impaired and need guidance when walking or someone to read your mail, this could help you satisfy the requirement for needing 'frequent help'. A test case in 1997 ruled that help needed with social activities can be taken into account. You can also get the allowance if you need continual supervision throughout the day to avoid putting yourself or others in substantial danger.

Night conditions

You will fulfil this condition if you are so disabled that you require prolonged (periods of at least 20 minutes) or repeated (at least twice nightly) attention during the night to help you with your bodily functions – for example, going to the toilet and getting in and out of bed. You can also get the allowance if another person needs to be awake for a prolonged period or at frequent intervals throughout the night in order to watch over you to avoid putting yourself or others in substantial danger.

Going into hospital

Page 15, second line of first paragraph should read 'After that, if you are single, your pension is usually reduced by £25.90...'. Second line of second paragraph should read 'When you have a dependant, your pension is reduced by £12.95 a week after six weeks in hospital.'

Backdating

In a number of places in Your Rights we refer to planned changes to restrict the time that benefit can be backdated to a maximum of one month. On 6 April 1998 the Government announced that it will not go ahead with these changes.

April 1998   FS/BU/98/03/01

Your Rights 1998-99 Budget Update

Incapacity Benefit
In general the Budget on 17 March 1998 did not affect the information in Your Rights 1998-99. However the Chancellor announced a package of measures to help disabled people who want to work. One proposed change is to remove the 16 hour limit on voluntary work for people receiving Incapacity Benefit. This is planned to come into effect in October 1998 and updates the section 'Work and Incapacity Benefit' on page 87.

Council Tax Benefit
On 27 March 1998 the Government announced changes to the restrictions to Council Tax Benefit for people living in properties in bands F, G or H (described in Your Rights on pages 55-56) which were introduced on 1 April 1998. There will now be protection for people entitled to benefit on 31 March 1998. In this situation benefit will not be restricted as long as people remain in the same property and do not have a break of entitlement of more than 12 weeks.

The mobility component

Although the mobility component is given to people who need help getting around, you can spend it how you choose. Remember that it is not available to people who become disabled after the age of 65.

You will receive the higher level if you are unable to walk or have great difficulty in walking because of a physical disability. The higher level is also available to people who are both blind and deaf and need someone with them when outdoors, to all people who have lost both legs at or above the ankle, and to certain severely mentally disabled people who have severe behavioural problems. If you can walk but need someone with you for guidance or supervision, you may be awarded the lower level.

Using a car

If you own a car and get the higher mobility component of DLA, you may not have to pay road tax. If someone drives a car for you, they can also apply for exemption from road tax. You will get details about this and about getting a car through the Motability Scheme when you first get the allowance.

You can also apply to the local authority for an orange badge which allows parking with some limitations but without charge at meters or where waiting is restricted. Some local authorities make a small charge for issuing the orange badge.

Examples of people who may receive DLA

Ellen Johnson is 62 and cannot walk very far owing to severe arthritis. Although she can manage to care for herself, she finds cooking very difficult because she cannot do tasks such as cutting, lifting and pouring. She applied for DLA and was awarded the higher level of the mobility component and the lowest level of the care component.

Albert Brown is 64 and suffers from dementia. During the day his wife or another relative stays with him all the time because he is very forgetful and sometimes wanders off or turns on the gas without lighting it. He normally sleeps all through the night. His wife applied for DLA on his behalf and he was awarded the middle level of the care component (because he needs supervision during the day) and the lower level of the mobility component because he needs guidance when outdoors.

Sarah Bloom is 68 and had a severe stroke six months ago which left her unable to walk and needing a lot of help, for example with washing, dressing and eating. Because she is 68 she is too old to claim DLA. She cannot get any help with her mobility needs but she can apply for Attendance Allowance because she needs personal care.

Remember that these are just examples and your situation is probably different. Whether you qualify for DLA, and if so at what level, will depend on your particular circumstances.

Rules covering both Attendance Allowance and Disability Living Allowance

If you are away from home

If you are receiving NHS treatment in a hospital, you cannot start to receive Attendance Allowance or DLA. However, you may receive either of these allowances if you are a private patient paying for the cost of hospital services.

If you are already receiving Attendance Allowance or DLA and you go into hospital, you will be able to continue to receive the allowance for up to four weeks. However, the allowance will stop sooner if your admission is within 28 days of a previous stay in hospital.

In the past, a stay in hospital did not normally affect the mobility component of DLA. However, the rules changed in July 1996. Some people in hospital for 12 months or more at the time of the change received transitional protection and can continue to get an amount equivalent to the lower rate of the mobility component.

For information about Attendance Allowance and DLA for people in residential or nursing homes, see pages 111–112. In general, a holiday abroad does not affect Attendance Allowance or DLA, nor do periods abroad for medical treatment. You should let your Benefits Agency (social security) office know when you intend to go abroad so that payment of the allowance while you are abroad can be considered.

How to claim

The claim forms for Attendance Allowance and DLA are quite long; the intention is that people can describe how their disability affects them. This means that a medical examination will not normally be necessary. Do not be put off by the length of the form. If you have difficulties filling it in, a friend or relative can fill in the form for you. A local advice agency may be able to help, or you can telephone the Benefits Enquiry Line for advice – the number is on the claim form. If it is difficult for you to get out, your local Benefits Agency (social security) office may be able to arrange for a visiting officer to call to help you with the form.

There are two main sections of the form: Section 1 deals with information about yourself and Section 2 asks about how your disability or illness affects you. At the time of writing there is also an 'Additional Section' asking for further information.

If you have difficulty with the second section or would rather have a medical examination, you can ask for a doctor to visit. Section 2 of the form and the Additional Section ask about the sort of help you need. Remember that it does not matter if you actually receive any help or not. Be sure to say what activities are difficult or impossible for you to do. For example, you may have to get dressed on your own because there is no one to help you but do explain if it takes a long time or if it is difficult – perhaps because you get out of breath. If you feel that having answered the questions you have not given a good picture of how your disability affects you, add any extra information you think would be helpful. If you have any problems with filling in the form, do ask for help. There is also a space on the form for your doctor or someone else who knows about your circumstances to complete.

If your claim cannot be decided from the information in the form, the Benefits Agency may ask for further information from someone such as your doctor or district nurse or they may arrange a medical examination. If an appointment is made for a doctor to visit, you may want a friend or relative to be there at that time. This will be particularly important if you have difficulty making yourself understood. The doctor, who will not be your own doctor but one appointed by the DSS, will probably examine you and ask further questions. It may be useful to make a note beforehand of the things you need to tell the doctor about when you need help or the difficulties you experience.

You can get the claim pack for Attendance Allowance or DLA from the local Benefits Agency (social security) office, or by telephoning the Benefit Enquiry Line on 0800 88 22 00 or by sending off the tear-off slip on leaflet DS 702 (Attendance Allowance) or DS 704 (DLA). You should return the form in the envelope provided within six weeks or you may lose some benefit.

When to claim

Although you normally need to fulfil the qualifying conditions for three months before you can start getting DLA and six months for Attendance Allowance, if you have only recently become disabled you should still apply as it may take some weeks to deal with your claim. If you are receiving a lower level of one of the allowances but your condition has deteriorated so you might now qualify for a higher level, you can ask for your case to be reviewed. You will need to satisfy the care or mobility conditions for the higher level for three months (DLA) or six months (Attendance Allowance) before it can be paid.

Effect on other benefits

Sometimes if you become entitled to Attendance Allowance or DLA this will also enable you to start receiving other benefits such as Income Support or Housing Benefit because these benefits can be higher if you are receiving a disability benefit. To ensure any benefit entitlement is backdated you may need to claim these other benefits at the same time as you claim Attendance Allowance or DLA. If you are not sure of your position get help from a local advice agency.

Terminal illness

People who are terminally ill can claim DLA or Attendance Allowance without the three-month or six-month waiting period. They will be considered to be terminally ill if they have a progressive illness that could limit their life expectancy to six months or less.

To claim ask your doctor for a DS 1500 report, which gives details of your condition. Send this in the envelope provided after completing Section 1 of the Attendance Allowance or DLA form, ensuring that you have ticked the special rules box on page 2. You do not need to complete the section which covers 'Help with personal care': if you are assessed as being terminally ill, you will automatically receive the higher rate of Attendance Allowance or the highest level of the care component of DLA. However, if you are under the age of 65 and you want to claim the mobility component of DLA, you will need to fill in the section on 'Help with getting around' and include this with your claim. Claims should be handled within 10–14 days and a medical examination will not normally be necessary.

An application can be made by another person on behalf of someone who is terminally ill with or without their knowledge, so it is possible for people to receive an allowance under the special rules without knowing their prognosis.

How it is paid

Attendance Allowance or DLA may be awarded indefinitely or for a set period, in which case it will be reviewed at the end of this time. Attendance Allowance is either paid weekly and collected at the Post Office or paid four-weekly in arrears directly into a bank or building society account. If you are receiving another benefit or pension, they will normally be paid together. DLA is normally paid four-weekly unless you were getting Attendance Allowance by weekly order book before April 1992. However, people claiming under the special rules because they are terminally ill can get weekly payments.

If you disagree with a decision

If you are refused an allowance or awarded a lower rate than you expected, you can ask for your case to be reviewed. It is best to ask for a review within three months of receiving the original decision. You should send in any additional written information that might help. A different adjudication officer will look at your case and may ask for extra evidence from people who know you such as your own doctor.

If you are not satisfied with the outcome of the review, you can appeal to an independent appeal tribunal against the decision. You should do this within three months of receiving the review decision. Your case will then go to a Social Security Appeal Tribunal if you are appealing against a non-medical decision such as whether you fulfil the residency conditions, or a Disability Appeal Tribunal if you disagree with a decision about whether you fulfil the attendance, supervision or mobility conditions. The Disability Appeal Tribunal will consist of three people not connected with the DSS, at least one of whom should be experienced in dealing with the needs of disabled people. If you wish to attend, you must request an oral hearing in writing, otherwise your case will be dealt with based on the written information you provide. At the tribunal you or a representative will be able to put your case as to why the decision should be changed.

If you want a review or appeal, you may find it useful to seek help locally and read the *Disability Rights Handbook* (see the 'Further reading' section for details about how to get a copy). The Government intends to make changes to the system of reviews and appeals and these are likely to come into effect in April 1999. Contact Age Concern for further information.

For Attendance Allowance see social security leaflet DS 702 and claim pack DS 2. For DLA see social security leaflet DS 704 and claim pack DLA 1. See also Age Concern Factsheet 34 *Attendance Allowance and Disability Living Allowance.*

INVALID CARE ALLOWANCE (TAXABLE)

This is a benefit for people who are unable to work full-time because they are caring for a severely disabled person for at least 35 hours a week. The benefit is not dependent on having paid NI contributions.

Do note that in some situations the person you care for could lose money if you start to receive Invalid Care Allowance (ICA). This will apply to a disabled person who receives the severe disability premium as part of their Income Support, Housing Benefit or Council Tax Benefit. See pages 40–41 for more information about the severe disability premium.

The weekly rates are:

Carer £38.70

Adult dependant £23.15

The person being cared for must be receiving one of the allowances referred to below, such as Attendance Allowance. They do not have to be a relative and may live separately or with the carer.

Who qualifies?

To qualify you must spend at least 35 hours a week looking after someone who is receiving Attendance Allowance (higher or lower rate), the care component of Disability Living Allowance (middle or highest level), or Constant Attendance Allowance of £42.00 or more paid with an industrial, war or service pension.

You must have started caring before the age of 65, although once you receive ICA it can continue to be paid after the age of 65. At the time of writing a claim can be backdated for three months but the Government intends that from June 1998 this will be restricted to one month. It is important to claim ICA even if the person you care for is still waiting to hear if they qualify for Attendance Allowance or DLA. You must also be resident in the UK and have lived here for at least 26 weeks out of the past 12 months.

You cannot get ICA if you earn more than £50 a week. The extra £23.15 which can be claimed for a dependent adult will not be paid if that person earns more than £23.15 a week, including any occupational or personal pension. It also may not be paid if they are receiving a State pension or benefit. When calculating earnings of the carer or their partner, certain work expenses are deducted.

Overlap with other benefits

If you are already getting £38.70 a week or more from certain other social security benefits or pensions, you may not be able to get ICA as well. This is because ICA 'overlaps' with some benefits including Incapacity Benefit, Retirement Pension and Widow's Pension.

If you have a spouse or partner who is claiming an addition to their benefit for you, that addition will be reduced by the amount of ICA received.

Example

Olive Zhukova is 62 and looks after her disabled mother, who gets Attendance Allowance. Olive's husband, Wilfred, is also ill and receives Incapacity Benefit with an addition of £38.70 for Olive. When Olive claims ICA of £38.70 a week, the benefit that Wilfred gets for her is reduced by the same amount (£38.70). This means that the benefit Wilfred gets for Olive is stopped altogether, although his own Incapacity Benefit continues to be paid.

However, if you have a low income it may still be worth claiming ICA even though it may not be paid in addition to your present benefit or pension. Although ICA is counted as income if you claim Income Support, Housing Benefit or Council Tax Benefit, people entitled to ICA may be able to get higher rates of these benefits, owing to the 'carer premium', as explained on pages 41–42.

Protecting your pension

If you are entitled to ICA, NI contributions will be automatically credited to protect your right to a future Retirement Pension unless you have retained the right to pay the married woman's reduced-rate contributions. If you receive another benefit instead and are not working regularly because you are caring for someone, you may get Home Responsibilities Protection (see pp 11–12).

When you reach pension age

When you reach pension age (60 for women, 65 for men), ICA will be adjusted to take account of any Retirement Pension you draw. If your pension is £38.70 or more, the allowance will stop. If your pension is less than £38.70, the allowance will be reduced by the amount of pension received.

If you are not entitled to a pension or do not claim one, ICA may continue.

If you are still receiving ICA at the age of 65, it can continue to be paid even if you are no longer caring for a disabled person.

See social security claim pack DS 700 or information leaflet FB 31 *Caring for Someone?* The Carers National Association produces information for carers. The address is Carers National Association, 20–25 Glasshouse Yard, London EC1A 4JS. Carers Helpline 0345 573369, weekdays 10.00 am–12.00 pm and 2.00 pm–4.00 pm.

STATUTORY SICK PAY (TAXABLE)

If you are an employee earning at least £64 a week and you are under 65, you will probably be entitled to Statutory Sick Pay (SSP) if you are off sick for at least four days in a row. This can continue for up to 28 weeks and it will be paid by your employer. The weekly rate is £57.70. You may also get sick pay from your employer's own scheme depending on the terms and conditions.

If you are unable to work because of sickness but not entitled to SSP, for example because you are self-employed or unemployed, you may be entitled to Incapacity Benefit, as explained below. If you have not paid enough NI contributions, you may qualify for Severe Disablement Allowance instead (see pp 90–91).

See social security leaflets NI 244 and NI 245.

INCAPACITY BENEFIT

This is a benefit for people who are unable to work owing to illness or disability. It was introduced on 13 April 1995 and replaced Sickness Benefit and Invalidity Benefit. It is based on NI contributions and is not means-tested.

The first part of this section covers the rules for people who make a claim on or after 13 April 1995. If you were receiving Invalidity Benefit immediately before that date, see pages 88–89.

Incapacity Benefit for new claimants

There are three levels of Incapacity Benefit. If you are an employee, you will probably be paid Statutory Sick Pay (SSP) by your employer for the first 28 weeks that you are unable to work (see above). However, if you are not entitled to SSP, for example because you are self-employed or unemployed, you may be able to get the short-term lower rate of Incapacity Benefit for up to 28 weeks. The short-term higher rate of Incapacity Benefit is paid from 29 weeks to 52 weeks of incapacity while the long-term rate is paid after 52 weeks. (People who are terminally ill or who receive the highest rate of the care component of Disability Living Allowance (DLA) will receive the long-term rate from 29 weeks.) The long-term rate can continue up to pension age as long as you remain unable to work. The short-term higher rate and the long-term rate are taxable, but the short-term lower rate is not. The weekly rates of Incapacity Benefit are:

Short-term lower rate £48.80

Short-term higher rate £57.70

Long-term rate   £64.70

If you become unable to work before the age of 45, you will receive an age addition which will be paid when you start to receive the long-term rate of Incapacity Benefit. There are two rates, depending on the age at which you become unable to work:

Under 35   £13.60

35–44   £6.80

Who qualifies?

To qualify for Incapacity Benefit you must fulfil the NI contribution conditions, be assessed as incapable of work and be under pension age (60 for women, 65 for men). If you have not paid enough NI contributions, you may qualify for Severe Disablement Allowance, as explained on pages 90–91.

The incapacity test

For the first 28 weeks of incapacity you will normally only need to provide a medical certificate from your doctor stating that you are unable to do your normal job, if you have one.

After 28 weeks, or from the start of incapacity if you do not have a job, most people will have to undertake an 'all work' test. This will involve a questionnaire and, in some cases, a medical examination, to decide whether you are incapable of any work – not just your normal job. However, you will not be subject to the incapacity test if you are terminally ill, receive the highest care component of DLA, are registered blind, or have certain severe medical conditions.

Increases for a husband or wife

The increase for an adult dependant can be paid only if your husband or wife is aged 60 or over (unless you are covered by the transitional rules for people previously receiving Invalidity Benefit). When this increase is paid with either of the short-term rates of Incapacity Benefit, the rate is £30.20 a week. However, this increase will not be paid if your husband or wife receives £30.20 or more from certain State benefits or from earnings (any occupational or personal pension they receive is counted as earnings). After 52 weeks the addition increases to £38.70 and the earnings limit to £50.35. If your husband or wife is receiving a State Pension or another benefit of £38.70 or more, you may not get the addition for them.

Work and Incapacity Benefit

You cannot receive Incapacity Benefit if you work unless it is of a 'therapeutic' nature undertaken on the advice of your doctor and with the approval of the Benefits Agency. The maximum you can earn is £48.00 a week after allowable expenses. With the exception of certain people working under medical supervision in a hospital or sheltered workshop, you cannot work for 16 hours a week or more. You may do voluntary work for up to 16 hours a week. If you do both voluntary work and therapeutic work, you can only do up to 16 hours in total.

When you reach pension age

The long-term rate of Incapacity Benefit cannot be paid after pension age (unless you were previously receiving Invalidity Benefit and had already reached pension age by 13 April 1995, as described below). So once you reach pension age (60 for women, 65 for men), you should draw the State Pension.

If you become incapable of work before pension age and are receiving short-term Incapacity Benefit, this can continue until you have been unable to work for up to a year. For people over pension age the short-term rate of Incapacity Benefit is £62.05 a week, although you may get less if you do not have enough contributions for a full Basic Pension. You may also receive Additional and Graduated Pension. There is an adult dependency increase of £37.20 which you may receive if your husband or wife is aged 60 or over – depending on any earnings, pensions or other benefits they receive.

How to claim

If you have been receiving Statutory Sick Pay (SSP), your employer will give you a claim form. If you have not been receiving SSP, contact your local Benefits Agency (social security) office.

If you disagree with a decision

If you disagree with a decision about your benefit, you can ask for your case to be reviewed or you can make an appeal to a Social Security Appeal Tribunal, as explained on pages 28–30.

If you were receiving Invalidity Benefit on 12 April 1995

If you were transferred from Invalidity Benefit to Incapacity Benefit in April 1995 and have continued to receive Incapacity Benefit since then, you will be covered by the transitional rules. These rules were introduced to provide some protection against changes which could reduce the amount of benefit people received. If you are covered by the transitional rules, your Incapacity Benefit will not be taxable.

How much benefit?

If you were receiving Invalidity Benefit on 12 April 1995, you would have been transferred to the long-term rate of Incapacity Benefit. The rates are:

Long-term Incapacity Benefit £64.70

Adult dependant £38.70

If you were receiving an increase for a dependent husband or wife with your Invalidity Benefit, this will continue to be paid on the same basis. The rules for payment of the adult dependency increase are the same as those for the increase paid with the State Pension, which are described on pages 4–5. If you make a claim for the dependant's increase now, the rules described on page 86 will apply, which means that your husband or wife must be aged 60 or over.

You may receive Invalidity Allowance if you were previously getting it with your Invalidity Benefit. The rates, which depend on the age at which you became unable to work, are:

Under 40	£13.60
40–49	£8.60
Men 50–59, women 50–54	£4.30

You may also receive an Additional Rate based on any entitlement to Additional Pension you built up between 1978 and 1991. However, the level of Additional Rate is frozen at the amount you were receiving with your Invalidity Benefit before April 1995 and will not be increased in future years. It also 'overlaps' with Invalidity Allowance, so your Additional Rate will reduce any Invalidity Allowance you are entitled to. The rules about working and Incapacity Benefit are the same as for new claimants and are described on page 87.

Incapacity test

There is a test of incapacity which involves completing a questionnaire, and in some cases, a medical examination, to assess whether you are able to do any work – not just your normal job. You will be exempt from the test if you received Invalidity Benefit without a break of more than eight weeks between 1 December 1993 and 12 April 1995 and were aged 58 or over on 13 April 1995. You will also be exempt if you are terminally ill, receive the highest rate of the care component of DLA, are registered blind, or have certain severe medical conditions.

Reaching pension age

If you were over pension age (60 for women, 65 for men) when Incapacity Benefit was introduced on 13 April 1995, you can continue to receive it up to the age of 65 (women) or 70 (men). You can choose to draw your State Pension instead, but once you do so you will not have the option of claiming Incapacity Benefit again. The State Pension is taxable but it does not have earnings limits and some people will receive more Additional Pension if they draw their State Pension.

If you were under pension age when Incapacity Benefit was introduced, it will stop at pension age. You should then claim your State Pension.

SEVERE DISABLEMENT ALLOWANCE (NOT TAXABLE)

This is a benefit for people who are unable to work for at least 28 consecutive weeks because of long-term disability or sickness and have not paid enough contributions to get Incapacity Benefit. The basic weekly rates are:

Claimant	£39.10
Adult dependant	£23.20

There are also additions for people who become unable to work before the age of 60; these are added to the basic rate of £39.10. The weekly rates are:

Under 40	£13.60
40–49	£8.60
50–59	£4.30

Who qualifies?

You must be under 65 when you first qualify and have been unable to work for at least 28 consecutive weeks. If you become incapable of work before the age of 20, you may qualify on this basis alone. If your incapacity starts after this age, you must also be medically assessed as at least '80 per cent disabled' for at least 28 consecutive weeks. In some circumstances you will automatically be treated as satisfying the 80 per cent disability condition, for example if you are registered blind or in receipt of certain levels of Disability Living Allowance. You also need to be normally resident in the UK and to have been living here for at least 26 out of the last 52 weeks.

Severe Disablement Allowance (SDA) 'overlaps' with certain other benefits, so if you are already receiving another benefit or pension, you may not get both. If your husband or wife is receiving an addition for you with his or her pension or benefit, then this may be stopped or reduced if you are awarded SDA.

If you apply on or after 13 April 1995, you can receive the adult dependency increase for your husband or wife only if they are aged 60 or over. If they have earnings over £50.35 or receive a State pension or benefit of £23.20 or over, you may not be able to get this increase. If you have been receiving the increase since before 13 April 1995 it can continue, even if your husband or wife is under 60.

You cannot receive both the full amount of SDA and a Retirement Pension. If you do not qualify for a Retirement Pension or it is less than SDA, you can continue to receive SDA to make your benefit up to the basic level of £39.10 plus the age addition if you qualify for one. You can continue to receive the allowance instead of drawing your pension.

See social security leaflet NI 252 or the SDA claim pack SDA 1.

OTHER BENEFITS FOR PEOPLE WITH DISABILITIES

This section gives brief information about other benefits for people with disabilities. More detailed information is given in the leaflets mentioned or you could look at the *Disability Rights Handbook* (see 'Further reading').

Disability Working Allowance (DWA)

This is a tax-free, non-contributory, income-related benefit for disabled people who are in work but have a limited earning capacity. To qualify you will need to:

- be in paid work for at least 16 hours a week;
- be at a disadvantage in getting a job;
- be receiving or have recently received one or more of certain disability benefits, including Incapacity Benefit, Severe Disablement Allowance and Disability Living Allowance; *and*
- have no more than £16,000 in savings.

If you fulfil these conditions, whether you receive DWA, and if so how much you can get, will depend on your income and savings and factors such as the people in your family.

If you give up Incapacity Benefit or Severe Disablement Allowance in order to work and draw DWA and the attempt at work is unsuccessful, you may be able to start drawing your previous benefit again if you claim immediately your work ceases, you are still incapable of work, and you last received your previous benefit within two years of your claim.

If you are considering giving up your disability benefit in order to work and claim DWA, it is a good idea to seek advice first. For more information contact the DWA Unit at Preston (see address on p 129) or a local Benefits Agency (social security) office, Jobcentre or advice agency.

See social security leaflet DS 703 and DWA 1 claim pack.

Industrial injuries scheme

The industrial injuries scheme can provide help to people who are disabled as a result of an accident at work or an industrial disease. The main benefit is Disablement Benefit, which can be paid in addition to other National Insurance benefits such as Incapacity Benefit or Retirement Pension. The level of payment depends on how disabled you are assessed as being. If you are awarded Disablement Benefit at the 100 per cent rate, you may also qualify for Constant Attendance Allowance if you need care and attention. There is also an Exceptionally Severe Disablement Allowance for those who are likely to need high levels of attention on a permanent basis.

See social security leaflets NI 2 (industrial diseases) and NI 6 (Disablement Benefit).

War Disablement Pensions and War Widows' Pensions

You may be entitled to a War Disablement Pension if you are disabled as a result of war or peacetime service in the armed forces. The amount awarded depends on how disabled you are. Civilians and certain other people, such as those in the Mercantile Marines, who are disabled by an injury due to war may also qualify for a War Disablement Pension. There are extra allowances which may be paid in addition to a War Disablement Pension. These include Constant Attendance Allowance for people needing a lot of care and attention because of their pensioned disablement and a Mobility Supplement if they have difficulty walking because of that disablement.

You may be entitled to a War Widow's Pension if you are the widow of someone whose death was due to service in the armed forces or an injury due to war. The amount paid depends on the rank of the person who has died and the age of the widow.

If you remarry, your War Widow's Pension will be withdrawn. Since 19 July 1995 a war widow who remarried but is widowed again or whose marriage has ended in divorce or judicial separation may now receive her pension again. The pension will normally restart from the date you claim. For a claim form or more information, ring the War Pensions Helpline on 01253 858858 or write to the War Pensions Agency (address on p 130).

The War Pensioners' Welfare Service has welfare officers who can offer help and advice to war pensioners and war widows who have problems about pensions or other matters. If you wish to consult a welfare officer, you should contact your nearest War Pensioners' Welfare Office. Your local Benefits Agency (social security) office will give you the address or you will find it in the leaflet mentioned below.

See social security leaflet WPA 1.

FINANCIAL PAYMENTS FOR INDEPENDENT LIVING

Support to enable people to live independently at home comes mainly through the provision of services, often supplied or arranged by the local authority. However, there are two types of cash payment that can be given to people to pay for the help they need: Independent Living Fund payments and direct payments from local authorities. Both have upper age limits.

The Independent Living Fund

The original Independent Living Fund was replaced by two separate funds: the Independent Living (Extension) Fund, which continues to make payments to people already receiving help at the end of March 1993, and the Independent Living (1993) Fund, which can make payments to new applicants. Both provide cash payments to enable severely disabled people to pay for personal care or household tasks in order to remain living at home.

You can be considered for help from the discretionary Independent Living (1993) Fund only if you are under the age of 66. You must also be receiving the highest care component of Disability Living Allowance, have no more than £8,000 in savings, be receiving Income Support or income-based JSA or not be able to afford the care you need from your income, and be receiving services from the local authority to the value of at least £200 a week.

Direct payments

Since April 1997 local authorities can give people cash payments as an alternative to directly arranging community care services. These payments will be available only to people who apply when they are under 65, but once you have been awarded direct payments you can continue to receive them after that age. The Government has said it will review who can receive direct payments.

There are restrictions about who the disabled person can employ. For example, you cannot use the money to pay a close relative in the same household.

For more information about the Independent Living (1993) Fund or direct payments contact your local authority social services department.

Other Financial Benefits

This part of Your Rights *gives details about other financial help that may be available for older people. It covers a variety of subjects including paying for fuel, health costs, Legal Aid, and help towards the fees for residential and nursing home care.*

Most, but not all, of the financial assistance outlined depends on your income and savings or whether you are receiving another benefit such as Income Support.

PAYING FOR FUEL, INSULATION AND REPAIRS

The cost of fuel is a major expense for most pensioners. This section outlines what help is available and the different ways to pay your bills.

Fuel debts

If you cannot pay your fuel bills, you may be threatened with disconnection. However, gas and electricity suppliers should ensure that if everyone in the household is a pensioner, the fuel supply will not be disconnected between 1 October and 31 March if you cannot pay. They must also follow set procedures before they can disconnect someone – for example, they must first allow you to choose the payment method which is best for you. If, after a reasonable period of time, you are still having difficulty repaying your debt, the company must offer to install a prepayment meter. You should check that the company is aware that you are a pensioner and also seek advice about making payments, as described below.

As soon as you realise that you cannot pay a fuel bill, you should contact the company concerned. Do not delay, as it will be much easier to sort out any problems before debts mount up. You can arrange with the gas supply or electricity company to pay a bill in instalments or have a prepayment meter installed. You may want to contact a Citizens Advice Bureau or a local Age Concern group for help in making arrangements with the company and to ensure that you can afford the agreed repayments.

'Fuel direct'

If you have a fuel debt and are receiving Income Support or income-based Jobseeker's Allowance (JSA), you may be able to avoid disconnection or get reconnected by going on 'fuel direct'. Some of your benefit will be withheld every week and paid direct to the company to cover the cost of fuel being used and the amount owed. If you think that too large an amount is being withheld, ask the local Benefits Agency (social security) office which administers your Income Support whether the company will accept a smaller amount.

Winter fuel payments

In November 1997 the Chancellor announced additional cash payments for pensioner households to help towards fuel bills for two winters. If you were receiving Income Support or income-based JSA, including one of the pensioner premiums, in the week starting 5 January 1998 you should have received £50 by the end of January 1998. A couple will have received one payment between them. If you were not getting Income Support that week but were over pension age (60 for women, 65 for men) and receiving a Retirement Pension or certain other benefits such as Attendance Allowance, you should have received £20 if you were the only qualifying pensioner in the household or £10 if you live with one or more qualifying pensioners. These payments were due to be paid by the end of March 1998. Payments will be made again in winter 1998–99 although at the time of writing full details were not available. Contact Age Concern England at the address on page 138 for more information.

Cold Weather Payments

If you receive Income Support or income-based JSA and it includes a pensioner or disability premium, you may be eligible for Cold Weather Payments. A payment of £8.50 is made when the average temperature at a specified weather station has been recorded as, or is forecast to be, 0° Celsius or below over seven consecutive days. Savings are not taken into account. These payments will be made automatically so you do not have to make a claim.

See social security leaflet CWP 1.

Paying your bills

Most electricity and gas customers receive their fuel before paying for it (ie on credit), with the amount used recorded by a 'credit meter'. Customers are sent their bills at the end of each quarter. If you find it hard to pay your bills quarterly, it may be easier to put aside some money regularly by putting it in a building society or post office savings account to earn some interest. Alternatively you can pay by a range of different methods, as outlined below.

Electricity and gas stamps

These stamps may be bought at outlets such as post offices or electricity shops. You cannot exchange the stamps for cash. Electricity stamps are no longer available in Scotland.

Regular payments

The gas supply or electricity company will estimate how much gas or electricity you will use over the next year so that you can make regular payments. The schemes available include paying by direct debit from your bank account, either quarterly or monthly, and a range of flexible payment and budget schemes which allow you to pay weekly, fortnightly or monthly.

At the end of the year, if you have paid too much, either you will get a refund or the amount overpaid will be credited to your account. If you have not paid enough, and the amount owed is small, it may be carried forward to the next year's payments. Otherwise, you will have to pay the difference.

Some gas and electric companies support payment through the PayPoint system. This is designed for people who prefer to pay their bills by cash on a weekly, fortnightly or monthly basis and has some advantages over other existing schemes. There is no transaction fee, and it uses a network of outlets such as petrol stations and off licences that are open for longer than normal hours.

Prepayment meters

The company may install a meter so you can pay for fuel as you use it. Coinless prepayment meters may be operated by tokens, keys or cards which can be bought from post offices, PayPoint outlets, electricity shops (formerly showrooms), some local shops or 24-hour vending machines in £5 (and sometimes £1) units. Coin-operated prepayment meters are operated by putting coins into a slot – but these are being replaced by coinless meters. Paying for fuel 'as you go' can be useful as a budgeting aid if you are on a low income as it allows you to regulate your use of fuel. However, fuel paid for by prepayment meter is usually more expensive both for the charge for the meter and also the unit cost of the fuel. If you pay your landlord for gas and electricity there is a maximum price they can charge so make sure that you are not paying too much. The Citizens Advice Bureau should be able to advise you on this. Prepayment meters can also be reset by the fuel supplier to pay off debt. If you are asked to pay for all or part of the cost of installing a prepayment meter and are receiving Income Support or income-based JSA, you may be able to get a loan or grant from the Social Fund for the installation charges (see pp 48–52 for more about the Social Fund).

See Age Concern Factsheet 1 *Help with Heating*.

Grants for insulation and draughtproofing

All householders aged 60 and over are eligible for a grant under the Home Energy Efficiency Scheme. Grants are available towards draughtproofing, insulating lofts, pipes, and hot and cold water tanks, cavity wall insulation, improvements to heating controls, energy efficient light bulbs and basic energy advice. If you do not have loft insulation or the existing material is less than 50 mm (2 in) thick, you can get a grant to insulate it with material up to 150 mm (6 in) thick. You can do the work yourself, use a 'network installer', such as a local energy project, or get the work carried out by a contractor.

For more information about the scheme and details of local network installers, telephone the Energy Action Grants Agency on 0800 181 667.

The size of the grant will depend on the work you have done and who does it. The maximum grant is £315. The full grant is available only to people receiving Income Support, income-based Jobseeker's Allowance, Housing Benefit, Council Tax Benefit, Disability Living Allowance, Attendance Allowance and Disability Working Allowance. People over the age of 60 not receiving any of these benefits will have to make a 75 per cent contribution to the cost with a maximum grant of £78.75.

The local authority can provide 'renovation' or 'disabled facilities' grants or 'home repair assistance' for improving insulation and heating systems. Home repair assistance and renovation grants given for this purpose are 'discretionary' – which means that it is up to the local authority to decide whether or not to give you the help.

Help with repairs and improvements

England and Wales

Home owners and some private tenants may be able to get a 'renovation grant' towards the cost of certain repairs or improvements from their local authority. This might include installing an inside toilet or a hot and cold water supply. These grants will depend on your income and savings.

All renovation grants are discretionary. The local authority should publish a 'private sector renewal strategy' explaining who will get priority for these grants.

'Home repair assistance', which is also discretionary, is intended to cover smaller items of work such as rewiring and insulating your home or minor adaptations. It is available to owner-occupiers, private tenants or housing association tenants. The maximum grant is £2,000 per application and £4,000 in any three years. Home repair assistance is available to anyone who is over 60 or is 'disabled or infirm'. Local authorities have considerable discretion in deciding who should get assistance.

'Disabled facilities grants' cover a variety of improvement and adaptation work intended to make life easier for someone with a disability. Some are mandatory and some discretionary, depending on the type of work needed. Disabled facilities grants will usually be mandatory if your home needs adaptations to enable you to get in and out of it or to use essential facilities, such as a bathroom, toilet or kitchen. They are also subject to an assessment of income and savings.

If you need help with repairs, improvements or adaptations, you should apply to the renovation grant section of your local authority. You should not start the work or buy any of the materials until you have received the local authority's approval to go ahead.

In some areas there are special agencies such as 'Care and Repair' or 'Staying Put' projects which give advice and practical assistance to home owners needing to repair or adapt their homes. Your local authority or local Age Concern group should know whether there is a scheme in your area.

See Age Concern Factsheet 13 *Older Home Owners: Financial help with repairs and adaptations.*

Scotland

The system of grants in Scotland is different, and not all grants are discretionary. For details of grants available in Scotland, contact your local authority or obtain Factsheet 13 from Age Concern Scotland.

PAYING FOR RESIDENTIAL AND NURSING HOME CARE

This section summarises the help you can get with residential or nursing home charges. Please note that the information in this section does not apply to people whose care in a nursing home has been arranged and paid for by the NHS and who are regarded as long-stay NHS patients.

There are different systems of financial support depending on when someone entered a home. The first part of this section looks at the rules for people entering a private or voluntary home on or after 1 April 1993 and the rules for those in local authority homes. The next part covers the position for someone who was already living in a private or voluntary residential or nursing home before 1 April 1993. There are then details about when Attendance Allowance, Disability Living Allowance (DLA) and Housing Benefit can be paid.

You should be aware that although there are national assessment and charging procedures, sometimes things do not run as smoothly as described here. For example there may be delays in obtaining an assessment or the local authority may not agree to take financial responsibility. If you have problems a local advice agency may be able to help.

Applying for a place in a residential or nursing home

This section explains the position for people who wish to enter a residential or nursing home or who entered a home on or after 1 April 1993.

If you wish to enter a residential or nursing home and you need help to pay the fees, you will need to be assessed by the local authority (the county, the metropolitan or London borough or, in some areas, the new unitary authority). The social services department (social work department in Scotland) will be responsible for arranging an assessment of your care needs. After this assessment, they will decide whether they can offer you help – either in your own home or in a residential or nursing home. Each local authority will have its own criteria for making these decisions. If you do not agree with its decision, you can make a complaint through the complaints procedure.

Private or voluntary homes

If the local authority agrees to arrange a place for you in a private or voluntary residential or nursing home, it will be responsible for paying the full fee to the home and assessing your income and savings to ascertain how much you must pay towards the fees. If you wish, you will be able to choose a different home (subject to certain conditions). If the home you choose is more expensive than the local authority thinks you need, then the local authority will arrange this as long as there is someone (such as a friend, relative or charity) able to make up the difference.

If there is no suitable place at the price the local authority would usually pay for someone with your assessed needs, they will be responsible for paying for a more expensive place to meet your needs.

Charging procedures

The capital limits are the same for both the local authority assessment and Income Support if you live permanently in a home. If you have more than £16,000 savings, you will have to pay the full fee until your savings reach £16,000. (See pp 106–107 for how your former home is treated.)

If you have £16,000 or less, you may be able to receive Income Support and/or financial support from the local authority towards the fees. You should apply for Income Support and local authority financial support at the same time. If you are already in a home apply for the support as your savings approach £16,000. Sometimes Income Support starts to be paid before the local authority starts funding. The income and savings rules for the Income Support and local authority assessments are broadly similar. If you have savings of £10,000 or less, these will be ignored; any savings between £10,000 and £16,000 will be counted as though you have an additional £1 a week income from every £250 (or part of £250) over £10,000. This is called 'tariff income'.

For Income Support your income will be assessed as described on pages 37–38. Your applicable amount will be calculated as on pages 38–42, plus an additional 'Residential Allowance' of £64 a week for homes in Greater London and £57.50 for homes in the rest of the country. Income Support will make your income up to your applicable amount.

The local authority will also assess your income and savings. From your assessed income (including tariff income), you will have to make a contribution towards the fees which will leave you with at least £14.45 a week for personal expenses.

Local authority homes

If you enter a home run by the local authority, you will not be able to claim ordinary Income Support or Residential Allowance. If your income is less than the Basic Pension and your savings are not more than £16,000, you may be entitled to Income Support to bring your total income up to the Basic Pension level. From this you would pay the local authority £50.25 per week, leaving you with £14.45 for personal expenses. If your income is more than the Basic Pension, you will have to pay more towards the fees, although you will still normally be left with at least £14.45 a week. You will have to pay the full fees yourself if you have savings over £16,000. The rules are the same for people who were already in a local authority home before April 1993.

Owning your home

If you are in a local authority home or the local authority has arranged a place in a private or voluntary home and you own your own home, its value will normally be taken into account, unless your stay is only temporary, or your partner lives there, or a 'relative' who is either disabled or aged 60 or over lives there.

For details about who counts as a relative in this situation and further information about the treatment of the former home, contact Age Concern for a copy of Factsheet 38 *Treatment of the Former Home as Capital for People in Residential and Nursing Homes.*

The local authority can, however, choose to ignore the value of your home if someone else lives there, for instance a friend aged over 60, or a relative or friend under 60 who has been caring for you for a substantial period. If the local authority says it will not use this discretion, you might want to complain through the formal complaints procedure.

If the local authority does not ignore the value of your former home, it will be able to place a 'charge' on its value, so that it can reclaim money owed to it when the property is sold. You should seek legal advice about this.

The local authority will also be able to take account of certain assets which you might have transferred to someone else in order to pay less for your care. It may be able to recover any debt from the recipients of such assets if the transfer was made within six months of the local authority arranging the funding of the place in the home. Even if the transfer was made more than six months before, the asset can still be taken into account. Further information is available in Age Concern's Factsheet 40 *Transfer of Assets and Paying for Care in a Residential or Nursing Home.*

For details about the system for people in local authority homes or needing local authority support in private or voluntary homes after 1 April 1993, see Age Concern Factsheet 10 *Local Authority Charging Procedures for Residential and Nursing Home Care.*

Couples

When one of a couple enters a residential or nursing home, the local authority will assess the amount that the resident has to pay towards the fees solely on the resident's income and savings. However, a spouse is considered to be a 'liable relative', which means that they may have an obligation to contribute towards the cost of care. An unmarried partner has no liability under the local authority charging procedures to pay for a partner's care.

The local authority has no power to insist on a means test of your spouse and, although some authorities may have developed their own formulae, there are no specific national rules about how much your spouse must pay. A spouse can be invited to make a contribution, and a voluntary agreement may be reached.

If no voluntary agreement is reached, the local authority can make a complaint to a Magistrates' Court (Sheriff Court in Scotland), which has the power to decide how much, if anything, a liable relative should pay.

If you have an occupational or personal pension and your spouse is not also living in residential care with you, the local authority will ignore half the pension when assessing your income if you pass at least this amount to your spouse.

The local authority can also use its discretion to vary the amount of the personal expenses allowance. For example, you might want to ask for this to be done if you are not married to your partner, as the local authority will not automatically ignore half of your pension in this situation.

The person at home may be able to claim benefits such as Income Support in their own right, depending on their income and savings.

See Age Concern Factsheet 39 *Paying for Care in a Residential or Nursing Home if you have a Partner.*

People living permanently in a private or voluntary home before 1 April 1993

If you were already resident in a private or voluntary residential or nursing home before 1 April 1993, you are covered by 'preserved rights' to the special higher levels of Income Support to help pay the fees. If you have savings of £16,000 or less, you may be entitled to help. If your savings are more than this, you will have to pay the full fees until they are reduced to this level. You should contact your local Benefits Agency (social security) office about claiming.

If, however, you are living in a home in England or Wales which caters for fewer than four people and you are meeting the full fees yourself, you will not normally have preserved rights to the special higher levels of Income Support. If you need help to meet the home's fees at some time in the future, you will need to go to your local authority.

The amount of Income Support you receive will depend on your income and savings, the type of home you are in and the level of fees charged. Savings between £10,000 and £16,000 will be counted as extra income of £1 a week for every £250 (or part of £250) over £10,000 – this is called 'tariff income'.

Income Support will bring your income up to the amount of the fees, subject to a national limit, which is generally £213 a week for residential homes and £318 a week for nursing homes. If the home is in Greater London, the limits will be increased by £44 a week for residential homes and £49 a week for nursing homes. There are higher limits for people whose physical disability began before they reached pension age (60 for women, 65 for men), and there is a higher maximum amount (£247) for someone in a residential home who is blind or who qualifies for the higher rate of Attendance Allowance or the highest level of the care component of DLA (see pp 70–81 for more details about these allowances). An additional £14.45 is also payable for personal expenses.

If the charges for a residential or nursing home are higher than the maximum amount that you can get from Income Support, the difference can be made up from your own savings or from other sources (for example relatives, friends, charitable assistance) without this affecting your benefit.

Example

Marion Black lives in a residential home outside London where the charges are £213 per week. She entered the home in 1992 and paid the fees from the money she received from selling her house. However, her savings are now down to £16,000 so she claims Income Support. Each week she receives a State Pension of £64.70 and an occupational pension of £30. Her Income Support is worked out as follows:

State Pension	£64.70
Occupational pension	£30.00
Tariff income from £16,000 savings	£24.00
Income Support towards fees	£94.30
Total	£213.00

In addition Marion will receive £14.45 for personal expenses. If the fees go up by £10, she will not get any extra Income Support because her income is already being brought up to the maximum level allowed. She will have to use her savings or the amount received for personal expenses, get help from friends, family or a charity, or find a less expensive residential home.

Owning your home

If you own your own home its value will normally be taken into account when your savings are assessed for Income Support.

However, this value will be ignored for 26 weeks, or longer if reasonable, if you are taking steps to sell it. The value of your home will also be ignored if your spouse or partner lives there, or a 'relative' who is either disabled or aged 60 or over lives in the property.

For more detailed information about the system of 'preserved rights' to Income Support, see Age Concern Factsheet 11 *Financial Support for People in Residential and Nursing Homes prior to 1 April 1993* and social security leaflet IS 50.

Attendance Allowance or Disability Living Allowance in a care home

The mobility component of Disability Living Allowance (DLA) is not affected by admission to a care home.

Whether or not you can receive Attendance Allowance or the care component of DLA will depend on the type of home you are in, when you entered it, and how the fees are being met.

Entering a private or voluntary home on or after 1 April 1993

If you are paying the full charges in a private or voluntary home, you can claim and receive Attendance Allowance or DLA provided you fulfil the other conditions (see pp 71–72 and 73–75). You can receive these allowances whether you arranged the admission yourself or the local authority arranged the admission.

If you need local authority financial support in order to meet the home's fees, you cannot start to receive Attendance Allowance or the care component of DLA. If you are already receiving one of these allowances, it will stop four weeks after the admission.

However, you may still retain an 'underlying entitlement' to the allowance. This means that if at a later date you move out of the home, or perhaps you sell your property and start paying the full fees yourself, you could start receiving the allowance again without making a fresh claim. You should contact the Benefits Agency and ask for the allowance to be paid again.

You may be able to receive one of these allowances if you claim Income Support as long as the local authority is not funding the fees in any way. The rules on this are different in Scotland so this applies only in England and Wales. Even here the rules may change, so for up-to-date information contact Age Concern England at the address on page 138 for a paper called *Paying for Residential and Nursing Home Fees from Income Support and Attendance Allowance.*

Living in a local authority home

If you receive Attendance Allowance or the care component of DLA and you move into a home run by the local authority, the allowance can only continue to be paid for up to four weeks whether or not you are paying the full fees yourself. If you are already living in a local authority home, you cannot start to receive one of these allowances.

Living in a private or voluntary home before I April 1993

If you were living in a private or voluntary home before 1 April 1993 and are paying the full charges yourself, you can claim Attendance Allowance or DLA provided you fulfil the other conditions (see pp 71–72 and 73–75). If you claim the higher rates of Income Support towards payment of the home's fees, Attendance Allowance or the care component of DLA will continue to be paid but will count as income and reduce the amount of Income Support that can be paid.

It may, however, still be beneficial to claim Attendance Allowance or the care component of DLA. If you qualify for £51.30 through Attendance Allowance or the highest care component of DLA, or you are blind, the fees of a residential home will be paid up to a maximum amount of £247 instead of the usual £213 maximum.

Housing Benefit in a care home

Most people in private and voluntary homes are not able to receive Housing Benefit towards a home's fees.

However, people may be able to claim Housing Benefit if they live in private or voluntary unregistered homes such as some Abbeyfield homes. Some others will be receiving Housing Benefit, for instance if they live in 'small' homes for three or fewer people and have not previously claimed the special rates of Income Support. If you are receiving Housing Benefit and living permanently in a care home, the lower capital limit may be £10,000.

People in local authority homes cannot receive Housing Benefit.

HELP WITH THE COUNCIL TAX

The Council Tax is the system of paying towards local government services in England, Scotland and Wales. The rates system continues in Northern Ireland. Under the Council Tax system all domestic dwellings are allocated to one of eight bands (A–H) depending on their estimated value in April 1991. The level of tax for a property in band H will be three times as high as the tax for a property in band A. One bill will be sent to each household. One or more people will be legally responsible for paying the bill, although the household can choose how to divide up the bill.

There are various ways that your bill may be reduced and these are summarised below. It may be possible to receive help from more than one of these schemes.

Exemptions Some properties, mainly certain empty ones, will be exempt, which means that there will be no Council Tax to pay. For example, your former home will be exempt if it is empty because you are living in a hospital or residential or nursing home, or because you have gone to live with someone else in order to receive or provide personal care. A property is also exempt if a severely mentally impaired person lives there alone and would be liable to pay the tax.

Disability reduction scheme The property may be placed in a lower band if it has certain features which are important for a disabled person such as extra space for a wheelchair or an additional bathroom or kitchen for the use of the disabled person. If your home qualifies for a reduction, your bill will be reduced to the level of tax for the band below the one your home is in. However, this will not be possible if your property is in the lowest band (A).

Discounts The Council Tax assumes that there are two or more people living in each property. A discount of a quarter (25 per cent) will be given if someone lives alone and a discount of half (50 per cent) will normally be given if no one is living there. However, some people will not be counted for the purposes of the Council Tax so discounts may still be given even if there are two or more people in a property. For example, someone who is 'severely mentally impaired' and some carers will not be counted.

Council Tax Benefit This depends on the income and savings of the person(s) responsible for the bill or the people they live with. It is described in more detail on pages 52–68.

Further information is available from Age Concern Factsheet 21 *The Council Tax and Older People*. If you live in Scotland, contact Age Concern Scotland for a factsheet.

HELP WITH HEALTH COSTS

Most of the treatment given under the National Health Service (NHS) is free, but there are some things for which most people have to pay part or all of the cost. This section first outlines hearing and chiropody services, which are free under the NHS. It then explains who can get help with the cost of other NHS services such as dental care, eye tests and glasses.

Free NHS services

Hearing aids

You should discuss hearing difficulties with your GP who may, if necessary, refer you to a hospital for tests. If you are prescribed a hearing aid, this will be fitted and issued by a local NHS hearing aid centre. NHS hearing aids are available on free loan; replacements and batteries are also free. It is possible to buy private hearing aids, but these can be expensive.

The Royal National Institute for Deaf People (RNID) produces a range of information leaflets on hearing loss and other matters concerning deafness. The address is RNID Helpline, RNID, PO Box 16464, London EC1Y 8TT. Tel: 0870 6050123. Textphone: 0870 6033077 (9.30 am–5.00 pm).

Chiropody

NHS chiropody services are free to everyone, but health authorities and GP fundholders vary in the extent of provision. Some are unable to provide a comprehensive service because of the pressures on financial resources. There may be a delay in being seen or a long wait between appointments. Recognising this, health authorities and GP fundholders traditionally give priority to certain vulnerable groups such as older people, people with diabetes and disabled people, whose clinical need for chiropody services is likely to be greatest.

To find out about your local NHS chiropody service, ask at your GP's surgery or telephone the NHS free telephone helpline on 0800 66 55 44.

Some people may wish to consider private treatment. Not all private chiropodists are State registered. The NHS employs only State-registered chiropodists (with the exception of fundholding GPs, who may not necessarily do so). Non-State-registered chiropodists have various forms of qualifications and training. If you go to a private chiropodist, you should enquire about their training. There are no regulations governing non-State-registered practitioners. Chiropodists who are State registered can use the letters 'SRCh' after their name. The local NHS chiropody service may keep a list of those State-registered practitioners who are in private practice in the area. The *Yellow Pages* may also list them.

Help with NHS costs

If you (or your partner if you have one) receive Income Support, you are entitled to receive help with the health costs described below by showing your order book or a letter from the Benefits Agency (DSS). If you or your partner receives Disability Working Allowance (DWA) or income-based Jobseeker's Allowance (JSA), you will receive the same help as described below for people getting Income Support. In the following paragraphs, therefore, wherever Income Support is mentioned it also covers these other benefits. Help may also be available to people receiving a war or Ministry of Defence pension in certain circumstances.

If you are not getting Income Support, DWA or income-based JSA but have no more than £8,000 savings, you can apply for help with health costs under the NHS Low Income Scheme. (People living permanently in residential or nursing homes have a different limit – £16,000.) If you qualify you will be sent one of two certificates. Certificate HC 2 entitles you to the same amount of help as people receiving Income Support. If your income is a little higher, you may get certificate HC 3, which may entitle you to more limited help. The certificates tell you how long they last, which will be six or twelve months. If you are aged 60 or over, the certificate will normally last for 12 months. To apply for a certificate under the Low Income Scheme, you can get form HC 1 from your local Benefits Agency (social security) office or NHS hospital; some dentists, opticians and GP surgeries also have them. It is best to apply in advance. Remember that if you receive Income Support, you do not need to apply for a certificate.

See Department of Health leaflet HC 11.

Prescriptions

NHS prescriptions are free to both men and women aged 60 or over. However, younger people can also get free prescriptions if they have a low income or suffer from one of a small number of 'specified medical conditions', which are listed in leaflet HC 11.

Prescriptions are free to people receiving Income Support and those who have certificate HC 2 on grounds of low income, as described above. People who have certificate HC 3 entitling them to partial help with some NHS costs cannot get help towards prescription charges.

If you cannot get free prescriptions, you may be able to save money by buying a prepayment certificate or 'season ticket'.

Dental care

NHS dental treatment, check-ups and dentures are free if you or your partner gets Income Support. Treatment will also be free if you have certificate HC 2 and the cost may be reduced if you have certificate HC 3. Details of how to apply for a certificate are given above. Every time you start a new course of treatment, tell the dentist that you are on Income Support or have a low income.

Unless you are entitled to free treatment or help with the costs, you will have to pay 80 per cent of the cost of most treatment up to a maximum of £340 for one course of treatment.

It is a good idea to make sure that you are registered with an NHS dentist for regular treatment (called 'continuing care'), as this means that you will be entitled under the NHS to any treatment that the dentist considers necessary to secure and maintain your oral health. Contact your local health authority (Health Board in Scotland) for advice on how to find an NHS dentist. Their number will be in the phone book.

● **No help is given towards private dental fees. If you want NHS dental care, make sure the dentist is providing you with NHS treatment before you start each course. You can do this when you discuss the proposed treatment with your dentist.**

Sight tests and glasses

Opticians may make a charge for a sight test. Some people are entitled to a free NHS sight test. You will qualify for a free NHS sight test if you or your partner receives Income Support or has certificate HC 2 as described above. Free tests are also available to people who belong to a priority group, which includes registered blind and partially sighted people, those who need complex lenses, and diagnosed diabetics. People who have glaucoma or someone aged 40 or over who is the parent, brother, sister or son or daughter of a person with diagnosed glaucoma will also qualify.

Look for opticians who display a sign that they do NHS sight tests because some opticians will provide only private sight tests. If you have certificate HC 3, as explained above, you may get some help towards the cost of a private sight test. If the certificate says that you can afford to pay less than the current cost of an NHS sight test (the optician will tell you how much this is), you should ask the optician for form GOS 5 on which you can ask for help with the cost of a private sight test. If this test costs more than the current NHS fee, you will have to pay the balance yourself, so it may be worth checking whether another optician might be cheaper.

If you cannot get to the optician's practice for a sight test, you may be able to arrange for an optician to visit you at home. If you are entitled to a free NHS sight test, you will not have to pay for the visit. The cost of a home visit may be reduced if you have certificate HC 3.

You are entitled to a voucher towards the cost of glasses provided you or your partner gets Income Support or has certificate HC 2. You may get some help if you have certificate HC 3. You may be able to claim a refund in some circumstances, if you do not receive your certificate in time, but it is better to apply well in advance. The voucher carries a financial value linked to your optical prescription; it may cover the full cost of the glasses or be used as part payment for a more expensive pair. If your glasses or contact lenses cost more than any voucher you are given, you will have to pay the difference. If you need complex lenses, you will be able to receive a voucher from your optician to help pay for the glasses regardless of income and savings. However, the amount of help will be greater if you or your partner receives Income Support or qualifies on grounds of low income.

Before you have a sight test or get glasses, find out whether you qualify for help. If you will have to pay for some or all of the cost, you may want to check whether another optician might be cheaper, as charges can vary.

Elastic hosiery, wigs, fabric supports

Elastic support stockings are available on prescription, and are free to both men and women aged 60 or over. Support tights are usually available only through the hospital service, and there may be a charge for these. However, they will be provided free of charge if you receive Income Support or have certificate HC 2; if you have certificate HC 3, you may get some help with the cost.

Wigs and fabric supports are supplied through hospitals and are free for in-patients. If you are an out-patient, there are charges depending on the type of wig or fabric support supplied. However, they are free if you are on Income Support or have certificate HC 2; if you have certificate HC 3, you may get some help with the cost.

Hospital travel costs

If you get Income Support, you are entitled to help with the necessary costs of travelling to and from hospital for NHS treatment. You may also get help towards these costs if you have certificate HC 2 or HC 3 on grounds of low income. See 'Help with NHS costs' above on how to apply for a certificate. If you are not sure what help you can get ask at the hospital before you travel.

If you are visiting a close relative in hospital and you are receiving Income Support, you may be able to get help with the cost of your fares from the Social Fund (see pp 48–52).

Medical care abroad

You are covered by the NHS only while you are in the UK. If you are abroad and fall ill, you may have to pay all or part of the cost of any treatment. There are special arrangements with European Union (EU) and some other countries which may enable you to get free or reduced cost *emergency* medical care abroad. If you are going to live in another country, you should find out well in advance about your entitlement to medical treatment there.

Before going abroad, get leaflet T6 *Health Advice for Travellers* from the local post office or by telephoning the Health Literature line (freephone 0800 555 777) to find out what cover there might be for treatment in the country you are visiting. It is advisable to take out private medical insurance to cover the full cost of any treatment you may need abroad whether you are going to an EU or non-EU country. Medical treatment is very expensive, as is the cost of bringing a person back to the UK in the event of illness or death.

● **No matter where you are going, check that you have enough travel insurance to cover any emergency expenses you may have to meet.**

For further information, write to the Department of Health, International Branch, Room 512, Richmond House, 79 Whitehall, London SW1A 2NS.

TRAVEL CONCESSIONS

Rail and underground

All rail companies must give one-third reductions on most types of ticket to people who have a Senior Railcard, which currently costs £18 (March 1998) and is valid for one year. It is available to people aged 60 or over provided proof of age is given. If you have a Senior Railcard, you can also buy a Rail Europ Senior Citizen's Card, which offers discount fares on rail travel in most of western Europe. Principal stations and travel centres should have the details of how to apply for these Railcards.

If you are disabled, you can buy a Disabled Person's Railcard, which currently costs £14, and allows you and a companion to travel at a third off most standard fares. Full details of who qualifies are given in a leaflet available from many local railway stations.

Underground or other transport systems may also offer concessions; you should ask at local offices.

Bus and coach services

In almost all areas of the country, pensioners qualify for some form of concessionary bus fare. Broadly there are four types of scheme:

- travel tokens which can be used for part or full payment of fares;
- flat-rate passes for any length of journey on one bus in a given area;
- half-fare passes, usually limited to off-peak, weekend and public holiday journeys;
- free bus travel passes limited to off-peak, weekend and public holiday journeys.

Apply to your local authority (London or metropolitan borough, district council or unitary authority) for details.

National Express has a Coachcard for people aged 50 or over.

It currently costs £8 a year and entitles the holder to discounts on fares. Other coach services may also offer discounts.

Taxicard schemes

These are available to disabled people in Greater London, who can obtain an application form from their local authority. At the time of writing, most passengers pay a flat fare of £1.50 per trip under the scheme plus any excess over £10.80 on the meter (a fare of £13 would cost £1.50 plus £2.20). Different rates apply in Bromley, Richmond, and Kensington and Chelsea.

There are extra small charges for luggage, additional passengers and travel at night, weekends and public holidays. An additional £7 is payable at Christmas and the New Year.

Taxicard schemes operate in Greater London with the exception of Barnet, Redbridge and Westminster, which run their own schemes. Greenwich does not participate in the London scheme nor does it have its own scheme.

There are also Taxicard schemes in some areas outside London – ask your local authority if they run a scheme.

Airlines

Some airlines may have concessionary fares for pensioners. Ask at the airline or travel agent for details.

Proof of eligibility

If you are drawing a pension but do not have a pension book (for example because your pension is paid into a bank account), you can get a card proving that you are a pensioner. Write, quoting your pension number, to the Pensions and Overseas Benefits Directorate, Tyneview Park, Whitley Road, Benton, Newcastle Upon Tyne NE98 1BA. If you have no proof of being a pensioner, you may have to produce a copy of your birth certificate or another official document showing your age.

See Age Concern Factsheet 26 *Travel Information for Older People.*

HELP WITH LEGAL FEES

If you need legal help, you may be able to get this free or at a reduced rate, depending on your circumstances and the type of legal problem you have. The Government is currently reviewing help with legal costs so there may be changes in the future.

Getting initial advice

The system whereby some solicitors offered a fixed fee interview is no longer running. However, there may be a locally based scheme in your area which offers an initial interview free or at a reduced price. For more information ask your solicitor or an advice agency such as the Citizens Advice Bureau.

Advice after an accident

To help people injured in an accident decide whether they can make a claim, the Law Society offers a free service called the Accident Line, which covers England and Wales. They will give you details of the Accident Line solicitor nearest to your home or work. You can then call the solicitor and arrange a free consultation at a time convenient for you. The Accident Line freephone number is 0500 19 29 39.

In Scotland the Law Society can arrange a free consultation with a local solicitor to help someone if they try to make a claim. Contact the Law Society of Scotland, 26 Drumsheugh Gardens, Edinburgh EH3 7YT. Tel: 0131-226 7411.

Legal advice and assistance scheme

England and Wales

If you are on Income Support or income-based Jobseeker's Allowance or have a low income and little or no savings, you may get free legal advice and assistance under the Green Form Scheme. A solicitor or Citizens Advice Bureau will be able to tell you whether you qualify for help. If you do, you may get a solicitor's advice, have letters written, have your case prepared for a tribunal (for example a Social Security Appeal Tribunal) or have other legal work done, provided it does not involve going to court or being represented at a tribunal by a solicitor. If you gain money or property as a result of the solicitor's work on your behalf, the solicitor must use this to pay his or her bill.

However, for most non-criminal (civil) cases in the Magistrates' Court or before a Mental Health Review Tribunal, a solicitor may be able to represent you under the Legal Aid advice and assistance scheme, called 'assistance by way of representation' (ABWOR). ABWOR is available for Mental Health Review Tribunals free of charge to patients, regardless of their financial circumstances.

Help with the cost of making a Will may be available through the Green Form Scheme if you are physically or mentally disabled or you are aged 70 or over.

Scotland

In Scotland you may be able to get 'Pink Form' advice and assistance from a solicitor. This will be free if you are on Income Support or income-based Jobseeker's Allowance and have little or no savings. Otherwise, you may have to pay a contribution. Nearly all legal work is covered, including wills, accidents and criminal matters. However, with some exceptions, representation by a solicitor in a court or tribunal is not covered under the scheme.

Legal Aid

England and Wales

If you are involved in a civil court case or a case which might lead to court proceedings, you should get advice from a solicitor, Citizens Advice Bureau or law centre about applying for a Legal Aid certificate. However, most civil cases in the Magistrates' Court are covered by 'assistance by way of representation', as mentioned above. You may be able to get Legal Aid if you qualify financially and the Legal Aid Board is satisfied that you have a good reason for bringing or defending the case. Even with Legal Aid you may have to pay a contribution towards the cost of your case. Legal Aid may not be available for a case involving a small amount of money.

If you gain money or property as a result of winning your case, you may have to pay some or all of your costs to the Legal Aid Board. This is known as 'the statutory charge'. The Legal Aid Board produces a leaflet called *Paying Back the Legal Aid Board*, which explains what the charge is and how it works.

It is also possible to get Legal Aid for some criminal cases. Check with a solicitor, Citizens Advice Bureau or law centre.

Scotland

Legal aid is available in Scotland for cases brought in the local sheriff courts or in the Court of Session in Edinburgh. If you want to bring a case, or contest a case brought against you, your solicitor can apply to the Scottish Legal Aid Board for legal aid. If you have a sound case, you may get free help if you are on Income Support or income-based Jobseeker's Allowance. Otherwise, you may have to pay a contribution, and this also applies if you have savings you do not need to live on. If you end up winning money or property, or manage to hold on to money or property you might otherwise have lost, you may have to contribute towards the cost of your case.

In criminal cases in Scotland, representation by a solicitor may be available under the criminal legal aid scheme (without having to pay a contribution) or under the assistance by way of representation scheme (either free or with a contribution).

For further information see the *Practical Guide to Legal Aid*, available from the Legal Aid Board, 85 Grays Inn Road, London WC1X 8AA. Tel: 0171-813 1000. The Scottish Legal Aid Board also publishes helpful leaflets on Legal Aid. Its address is 44 Drumsheugh Gardens, Edinburgh EH3 7SW. Tel: 0131-226 7061.

See also Age Concern Factsheet 43, *Obtaining and Paying for Legal Advice*.

Further Information

This part of Your Rights *gives details about local and national sources of help to contact for assistance and advice. In addition, there is information about ordering DSS social security leaflets, Age Concern factsheets, and other publications on social security benefits mentioned in the book. Also included is an index to help you find the information you require in this book.*

BENEFITS AGENCY/DEPARTMENT OF SOCIAL SECURITY

The Department of Social Security (DSS) is the Government department responsible for pensions and social security benefits. The levels of payments and the rules for pensions and benefits are set by Parliament but the administration of pensions and benefits is dealt with by the Benefits Agency, which is described as an 'executive agency of the DSS'.

A local library or post office will tell you the address of your local Benefits Agency office, or you can look in the telephone book where it will be under 'Benefits Agency' or 'Social Security'. You can contact your local office by telephone, by letter or by calling in. If you have difficulties getting out, you can ask for a visiting officer to come and see you.

If you have a problem with the administration of a benefit – for example there is a delay in processing your claim – you can telephone or write to the Customer Service Manager at your local office. Social security leaflet BAL 1 *Tell Us About It* tells you how to complain or make comments on the service you receive. If you are still dissatisfied, get in touch with a local advice agency or your MP.

National Benefits Agency/DSS addresses

Pensions and Overseas Benefits Directorate
Tyneview Park
Whitley Road
Benton
Newcastle Upon Tyne
NE98 1BA

For help and advice about the State Retirement Pension or Widow's Benefit paid by automated credit transfer (ACT), telephone 0191-203 0203 7.00am–7.00pm weekdays. Textphone for the deaf or hard of hearing 0191-201 0194.

For information about benefits payable abroad, telephone 0191-218 7777, 7.30am–4.30pm weekdays. Textphone for the deaf or hard of hearing 0191-218 7280.

Disability Benefits Unit
Warbreck House
Warbreck Hill Road
Blackpool FY2 0YE
Tel: 0345 123456
Textphone: 0345 224433
7.30am–6.30pm weekdays

The Disability Benefits Unit administers Disability Living Allowance and Attendance Allowance although initial claims are normally dealt with at the regionally based Disability Benefit Centres.

Disability Working Allowance Unit
Freepost PR1211
Preston
Lancashire PR2 2TF
Tel: 01772 883300

Invalid Care Allowance Unit
Palatine House
Lancaster Road
Preston
Lancashire PR1 1HB
Tel: 01253 856123

Benefit Enquiry Line and Form Completion

For advice and information about disability benefits telephone 0800 88 22 00. Textphone (for deaf people) 0800 24 33 55.

For the form completion service, which covers disability benefits including Attendance Allowance and Disability Living Allowance, telephone 0800 44 11 44 8.30am–6.30pm weekdays, 9.00am–1.00pm Saturdays.

War Pensions Helpline

War Pensions Agency
Norcross
Blackpool FY5 3WP

For general advice on war pensions telephone 01253 858858, 8.15am–5.15 pm Mondays to Thursdays, 8.15am–4.30pm Fridays.

LOCAL SOURCES OF HELP

Age Concern (Old People's Welfare)

Most areas have an Age Concern or Old People's Welfare group which provides services and advice. You can find the address from the phone book, library or Citizens Advice Bureau, or you can write to the appropriate national Age Concern (addresses on p 138) for the address of your nearest group.

Citizens Advice Bureau (CAB)

The local offices provide advice and information on all kinds of subjects including social security benefits, housing and consumer problems. You can find out where your nearest CAB is from the phone book or at your local library.

Law centre

There may be a law centre giving free legal advice in your area. Check in the telephone book or at a Citizens Advice Bureau, or telephone the Law Centres Federation (0171-387 8570).

Local authority/council

In England the structure of local government depends on whether you live in a county, or in a metropolitan or London borough or one of the new unitary authorities. All areas in Scotland and Wales have a unitary authority. In England, if you live in a county, the district council will deal with Housing Benefit, Council Tax Benefit and other matters to do with the Council Tax. You will need to contact the county council about social services. In a metropolitan or London borough or unitary authority there will be just one authority that will deal with the Council Tax, Housing Benefit and social services. Some authorities have welfare rights workers to advise on benefits. You will find the address of your local authority in the telephone book under the name of your county, unitary authority, metropolitan or London borough, or ask at your local library.

Local councillor

A councillor for your area may be able to help with problems with the local authority. You can get the names of the councillors for your 'ward' from the town hall, library or Citizens Advice Bureau.

Local Government Ombudsman

If you feel you have suffered because of maladministration in the way the local authority has dealt with your case, you can make a complaint to the Local Government Ombudsman. You can do this direct or through your local councillor. Ask a local advice agency or councillor for further information.

Member of Parliament (MP)

Your MP may be able to help with problems involving Government departments. If you do not know who your MP is, ask at the town hall, library or Citizens Advice Bureau. Most MPs hold regular surgeries locally; or you can write to your MP at the House of Commons, London SW1A 0AA.

For a complaint about unfair treatment by a Government department (for example a delay with a claim for a social security benefit), ask the MP to refer your complaint to the Parliamentary Ombudsman.

Trade union

If you were a member of a trade union before retirement, it may be worth contacting your local branch, particularly for problems over a pension from work.

Welfare rights and money advice centres

There may be an independent welfare rights or money advice centre locally. Money advice centres generally deal with debt problems and may accept referrals only from other agencies.

NATIONAL SOURCES OF HELP

The national organisations listed below may be able to help or put you in touch with a source of advice.

Carers National Association

20–25 Glasshouse Yard
London EC1A 4JS
Tel: 0171-490 8818

Helpline: 0345 573369, weekdays 10.00am–12.00pm and 2.00pm–4.00pm

Child Poverty Action Group

4th Floor
1–5 Bath Street
London EC1V 9PY
Tel: 0171–253 3406

Counsel and Care

Twyman House
16 Bonny Street
London NW1 9PG
Tel: 0171-485 1566

Local rate call: 0845 300 7585 weekdays 10.30am–4.00pm.

Disability Alliance

1st Floor East
Universal House
88–94 Wentworth Street
London E1 7SA
Tel: 0171-247 8776

Energy Action Grants Agency

Eldon Court
Eldon Square
Newcastle Upon Tyne NE1 7HA
Tel: 0800 181 667

Pensions Advisory Service

11 Belgrave Road
London SW1V 1RB
Tel: 0171–233 8080

Royal National Institute for the Blind

224 Great Portland Street
London W1N 6AA
Tel: 0171-388 1266

Royal National Institute for Deaf People

RNID Helpline
RNID
PO Box 16464
London EC1Y 8TT
Tel: 0171-296 8000 (general)

Helpline: 0870 6050123, 9.30 am–5.30 pm

Textphone: 0870 6033007

For information about national organisations in Scotland, Wales and Northern Ireland, contact the appropriate national Age Concern (addresses on p 138).

FURTHER READING

Age Concern factsheets

Age Concern produces around 40 factsheets covering a wide range of subjects, some of which have been mentioned in *Your Rights*. Single copies are available free. To receive any of these or a complete list of factsheets send an sae (9" × 6") to Age Concern England, Wales or Scotland (addresses on p 138 or ring 0800 00 99 66).

Benefits Agency/DSS leaflets

As well as the leaflets mentioned in *Your Rights*, there is a catalogue of all the social security leaflets produced (Cat 1). Social security leaflets should be available from your local Benefits Agency (social security) office, and they are sometimes in libraries, post offices or CABs. Alternatively you can write to: The Stationery Office, The Causeway, Oldham Broadway Business Park, Chadderton, Oldham OL9 0XD. Leaflets on help with health costs are available from the Department of Health, Two Ten, PO Box 410, Wetherby LS23 7LN.

Other publications

For detailed information on services and benefits for disabled people, you may wish to get the *Disability Rights Handbook*, £11 (£7 for individuals receiving any State benefits), available from the Disability Alliance, 1st Floor East, Universal House, 88–94 Wentworth Street, London E1 7SA.

For detailed information on all social security benefits, with reference to the relevant Government legislation, you may wish to refer to the *National Welfare Benefits Handbook* (income-related benefits), £8.95 (£3 for benefit claimants), and the *Rights Guide to Non-Means-Tested Social Security Benefits*, £8.95 (£3 for benefit claimants). For detailed information about Jobseeker's Allowance see the *Jobseeker's Allowance Handbook*, £8.95 (£3 for benefit claimants). These books can be ordered from the Child Poverty Action Group, 1–5 Bath Street, London EC1V 9PY. They may also be available for reference at your local library.

Keeping up to date

Your Rights is based on the information available at the beginning of March 1998 and the benefit levels will normally apply until the first week in April 1999. A new edition of the book will be published next year to cover the period from April 1999 to April 2000. However, sometimes changes are made during the course of a year.

If you would like us to inform you of any major changes introduced before April 1999, please cut off this page and return it to the address below.

Write in with your details if you do not want to cut up the book.

Dear Age Concern

Please send me details about any major changes introduced before April 1999

Name (block letters) _____

Signature _____

Address _____

_____

_____

Postcode _____

Please return to:

Mail Order Unit
Age Concern England
1268 London Road
London SW16 4ER

ABOUT AGE CONCERN

Your Rights: A guide to money benefits for older people is one of a wide range of publications produced by Age Concern England – the National Council on Ageing. In addition, Age Concern England is actively engaged in training, information provision, research and campaigning for retired people and those who work with them. It is a registered charity dependent on public support for the continuation of its work.

Age Concern England links closely with Age Concern organisations in Scotland, Wales and Northern Ireland to form a network of over 1,400 independent local UK groups. These groups, with the invaluable help of an estimated 250,000 volunteers, aim to improve the quality of life for older people and develop services appropriate to local needs and resources. These include advice and information, day care, visiting services, transport schemes, clubs and specialist facilities for physically and mentally frail older people.

Age Concern England
1268 London Road
London SW16 4ER
Tel: 0181-679 8000

Age Concern Scotland
113 Rose Street
Edinburgh EH2 3DT
Tel: 0131-220 3345

Age Concern Cymru
4th Floor
1 Cathedral Road
Cardiff CF1 9SD
Tel: 01222 371566

Age Concern Northern Ireland
3 Lower Crescent
Belfast BT7 1NR
Tel: 01232 245729

PUBLICATIONS FROM AGE CONCERN BOOKS

Money matters

Your Taxes and Savings 1998–99
Sally West and the Money Management Council
The definitive annual guide to financial planning for older people, this popular book:

- is fully revised and updated
- explains the tax system in clear, concise language
- describes the range of saving and investment options available
- includes model portfolios to illustrate a range of financial scenarios

Your Taxes and Savings explains how the tax system affects people over retirement age, including how to avoid paying more tax than necessary.

£4.99   0-86242-256-6

Using Your Home as Capital 1998–99
Cecil Hinton
This best-selling book for home owners, which is updated annually, gives a detailed explanation of how to capitalise on the value of your home and obtain a regular additional income.

£4.99   0-86242-258-2

The Pensions Handbook 1998–99: The pensions system explained
Sue Ward
Many older people in their later working lives become concerned about the adequacy of their existing pension arrangements. This annually updated title addresses these worries and suggests strategies to enhance the value of a prospective pension.

£6.99   0-86242-257-4

General

Changing Direction: Employment options in mid-life
Sue Ward
Redundancy or early retirement can come as a shock to anybody, but the impact in mid-life can be devastating. This topical and highly practical book is designed to help those aged 40–55 get back to work. Always positive and upbeat, it examines issues such as adjusting to change, finances, opportunities for work, deciding what work you really want to do and working for yourself.
£9.99 0-86242-190-X

The Retirement Handbook
Caroline Hartnell
A comprehensive handbook for older people on the point of retirement, this book is full of practical information and advice on all the opportunities available. It also points readers in the right direction to obtain more information when required. Drawing on Age Concern's wealth of experience, it covers everything you need to know, including:

- managing your money
- staying healthy
- using your time
- leisure activities
- housing options
- relationships

The *Retirement Handbook* is easy to use and designed to encourage everyone to view retirement as an opportunity not to be missed.
£7.99 0-86242-237-X

Healthy Eating on a Budget
Sara Lewis and Dr Juliet Gray
Opening with a comprehensive introduction to achieving a nutritionally balanced diet, this book contains 100 plus closely costed recipes for the health-conscious cook, all of which are flagged up to show their nutritional values and calorie content.
£6.95 0-86242-170-5

Health and care

The Carers Handbook Series

The Carers Handbook Series has been written for the families and friends of older people. It guides you through the key stages of a crisis and helps you take practical, informed decisions.

Caring for Someone with an Alcohol Problem
Mike Ward

More people drink alcohol than smoke, gamble or use illegal drugs. When drinking becomes a problem, the consequences for the carer can often be so physically and emotionally exhausting that it is difficult to see any way out of the situation. This book will be of invaluable help to anyone who lives with or cares for a problem drinker, with particular emphasis on the problems of caring for an older problem drinker.
£6.99 0-86242-227-2

Caring for Someone at a Distance
Julie Spencer-Cingöz

People are now living longer than at any previous time in history, and this means that, sooner or later, we are likely to find ourselves looking after a loved one or a friend – often at a distance. This book will help you to identify the needs and priorities that have to be addressed, offering guidance on the key decisions to be made, minimising risks, what to look for when you visit, how to get the most out of your visits, dealing with your relative's finances and keeping in touch.
£6.99 0-86242-228-0

The Carer's Handbook: What to do and who to turn to
Marina Lewycka

At some point in their lives millions of people find themselves suddenly responsible for organising the care of an older person with a health crisis. All too often such carers have no idea what services are available or who can be approached for support. This book is designed to act as a first point of reference in just such an emergency, signposting readers on to many more detailed, local sources of advice.
£6.99 0-86242-262-0

Finding and Paying for Residential and Nursing Home Care
Marina Lewycka
Acknowledging that an older person needs residential care often represents a major crisis for family and friends. Feelings of guilt and betrayal invariably compound the difficulties faced in identifying a suitable care home and sorting out the financial arrangements. This book provides a practical step-by-step guide to the decisions which have to be made and the help which is available.
£6.99   0-86242-261-2

Caring for Someone who is Dying
Penny Mares
Confronting the knowledge that a loved one is going to die soon is always a moment of crisis. And the pain of the news can be compounded by the need to take responsibility for the care and support given in the last months and weeks. This book attempts to help readers cope with their emotions, identify the needs which the situation creates and make the practical arrangements necessary to ensure that the passage through the period is as smooth as possible.
£6.99   0-86242-260-4

Caring for Someone who has Dementia
Jane Brotchie
Caring for someone with dementia can be physically and emotionally exhausting, and it is often difficult to think about what can be done to make the situation easier. This book shows how to cope better and seek further help as well as containing detailed information on the illness itself and what to expect in the future.
£6.99   0-86242-259-0

Caring for Someone who has had a Stroke
Philip Coyne with Penny Mares
Supportive and positive, this book is designed to help carers understand stroke and its immediate aftermath and contains extensive information on hospital discharge, providing care, rehabilitation and adjustment to life at home.
£6.99   0-86242-264-7

Choices for the Carer of an Elderly Relative
Marina Lewycka

Being a carer may mean many different things – from living at a distance and keeping a check on things by telephone to taking on a full-time caring role. This book looks at the choices facing someone whose parent or other relative needs care. It helps readers to look at their own circumstances and their own priorities and decide what is the best role for themselves – as well as the person being cared for.
£6.99 0-86242-263-9

If you would like to order any of these titles, please write to the address below, enclosing a cheque or money order for the appropriate amount made payable to Age Concern England. Credit card orders may be made on 0181-679 8000.

Mail Order Unit
Age Concern England
1268 London Road
London SW16 4ER

ACE Books Catalogue 1998/99

A new edition of the ACE Books Catalogue has just been printed. It gives an up-to-date listing of all Age Concern books, which contain information and specialist advice for the over 50s and those working with them.

Topics include money matters, health and care, housing, a range of books aimed at professionals working with older people, and research and policy titles.

If you would like a copy, please fill out the form below and return it freepost to the address below. Please photocopy the form if you do not wish to cut up the book.

Please send me _____ copies of the ACE Books Catalogue 1998/99 (Free of charge)

Name (block letters) _____

Title _____

Organisation _____

Address _____

_____

Postcode _____ **Telephone** _____

Please return to:

Mail Order Department
Age Concern England
FREEPOST
London SW16 4BR   (no stamp required)

Tel: 0181-765 7203   Fax: 0181-679 6069
E-mail: mail.order@ace.org.uk

Bound – to last longer

We are often complimented on how easy *Your Rights* is to read and use. But as so many people use the book so often, it can become dog-eared, and even damaged.

That's why some of our regular users have asked if we can produce a tough, spiral-bound 'professional' edition of *Your Rights*. This seems like a good idea, although, naturally, it would be more expensive.

Would you be interested?

Please let us know your views by ticking one of the boxes and returning the form freepost to the address below. Please photocopy the form if you do not wish to cut up the book.

☐ **YES!** I would be interested in a spiral-bound copy of *Your Rights*. Contact me if you publish a professional edition.

☐ **NO.** I don't need a tougher, spiral-bound edition of *Your Rights*.

Name (block letters) _____

Title _____

Organisation _____

Address _____

_____

Postcode _____   **Telephone** _____

Please return to:

Publishing Department
Age Concern England
FREEPOST
London SW16 4BR   (no stamp required)

Tel: 0181-765 7455   Fax: 0181-764 6594
E-mail: books@ace.org.uk

INDEX

and home owners 106–107
and Housing Benefit 53,
112–113
local authority 106
private or voluntary 105–106
residents before 1 April 1993
109–111, 112
Retirement Pensions
(*see* Additional, Basic,
Graduated, occupational
and personal pensions)
Reviews of pensions 15, 28

S
Savings 35
Secretary of State decisions 30
Self-employment 8
Separated women 6
SERPS 16–18
Service charges 54–55
Severe Disablement Allowance
90–91
Sight tests 118, 119
Social Fund payments 48–52
Social Security Appeal Tribunal
(SSAT) 28, 29
Spectacles 118–119
Statutory Sick Pay 84, 85
Support stockings, elastic 119

T
'Tariff income' 36, 109
Taxicard schemes 122

Trade unions 132
Travel concessions 121–122

U
Underground fares 121
Unemployment benefits 22–24,
25

V
Voluntary contributions 10

W
War Disablement Pensions 93
War Pensions Agency 130
War Widows' Pensions 93
Water rates 54
Widowers
Additional Pensions 18
Graduated Pensions 19
Retirement Pensions 7
Widows
Additional Pensions 18, 26
Graduated Pensions 19, 26
and remarriage 7, 26
Retirement Pensions 6–7
War Widows' Pensions 93
Widows' Payments 25–26
Widows' Pensions 21, 26
Wigs 119
Wills, making 124
'Working life' 9

BENEFIT RATES APRIL 1998-99

Some of the main weekly benefit rates are listed below for quick reference:

Attendance Allowance
higher rate	£51.30
lower rate	£34.30

Disability Living Allowance
care component	highest rate	£51.30
	middle rate	£34.30
	lowest rate	£13.60
mobility component	higher rate	£35.85
	lower rate	£13.60

Income Support/Housing Benefit/Council Tax Benefit standard applicable amounts for people aged 60 or over*

age 60–74	single person	£70.45
	couple	£109.35
age 75–79	single person	£72.70
	couple	£112.55
aged 80+ or 60+ and disabled	single person	£77.55
	couple	£117.90

Invalid Care Allowance	£38.70
Incapacity Benefit (long-term rate)	£64.70
Severe Disablement Allowance (basic rate)	£39.10

Retirement pension
basic rate	£64.70
wife on husband's contributions	£38.70
couple on husband's contributions	£103.40

*See pages 38–45 for explanations of how applicable amounts are calculated and details of other premiums and housing costs which may give rise to higher rates.